Dychweler/adnewydder erbyn y dyddiad olaf
uchod
Please return/renew this item by the last date
shown

CYNGOR
Sir Ddinbych
Denbighshire
COUNTY COUNCIL

Gwasanaeth Llyfrgell Sir Ddinbych
Denbighshire Library Service

Credits

Footprint credits
Editor: Stephanie Rebello
Production and layout: Emma Bryers
Maps: Kevin Feeney
Cover: Pepi Bluck

Publisher: Patrick Dawson
Managing Editor: Felicity Laughton
Advertising: Elizabeth Taylor
Sales and marketing: Kirsty Holmes

Photography credits
Front cover: Robcsee/Shutterstock.com
Back cover: Zvonimir Atletic/
Shutterstock.com

Printed in Great Britain by CPI Antony Rowe,
Chippenham, Wiltshire

MIX
Paper from
responsible sources
FSC® C013604
www.fsc.org

Publishing information
Footprint *Focus Istria & Kvarner*
1st edition
© Footprint Handbooks Ltd
March 2013

ISBN: 978 1 909268 14 2
CIP DATA: A catalogue record for this book
is available from the British Library

® Footprint Handbooks and the Footprint
mark are a registered trademark of
Footprint Handbooks Ltd

Published by Footprint
6 Riverside Court
Lower Bristol Road
Bath BA2 3DZ, UK
T +44 (0)1225 469141
F +44 (0)1225 469461
footprinttravelguides.com

Distributed in the USA by Globe Pequot
Press, Guilford, Connecticut

The content of Footprint *Focus Istria &
Kvarner* has been taken directly from
Footprint's *Croatia* handbook which was
researched and written by Jane Foster.

Every effort has been made to ensure that
the facts in this guidebook are accurate.
However, travellers should still obtain advice
from consulates, airlines, etc. about travel
and visa requirements before travelling.
The authors and publishers cannot accept
responsibility for any loss, injury or
inconvenience however caused.

LLYFRGELLOEDD SIR DDINBYCH	
C46 0000 0525 892	
Askews & Holts	14-Jan-2014
914.972	£5.99
DE	

Contents

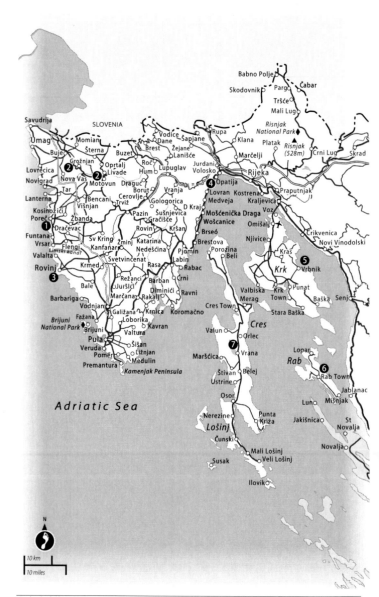

The large, triangular peninsula of Istria has an identity all of its own. Historically it has close ties with Italy and many towns, especially on the western side, are still bilingual. Dubbed the 'Tuscany of Croatia', its restaurants serve beautifully presented creative cuisine, farmhouses dish up local specialities and offer accommodation, and the tourist board has set up bike paths and wine roads.

On the tip of the peninsula, the region's principal city and port is Pula, with a first-century Roman forum as the main square and an ancient amphitheatre dominating the skyline. Close by are the islands of Brijuni National Park, which once served as the summer residence of the late President Tito.

On the west coast, the resort town of Poreč is home to a splendid sixth-century basilica decorated with stunning Byzantine mosaics, while neighbouring Rovinj is made up of ochre- and russet-coloured houses clustered around a pretty fishing harbour.

Moving inland to the Heart of Istria, narrow country roads meander through a gently rolling landscape of woodland and vineyards. In the lovely fortified hill towns of Motovun and Grožnjan you'll find a medieval ambience and some excellent gourmet eateries.

The Kvarner Gulf, a large deep bay sheltered by mountains, is presided over by Rijeka, a slightly austere industrial port. West is Opatija, Croatia's oldest coastal resort, packed with grandiose, Austro-Hungarian-style hotels. East, Risnjak National Park offers dense pine forests, mountain air, hiking and skiing.

Krk, linked to the mainland by bridge, has Romanesque churches in Krk Town, a pretty monastery on the islet of Košljun and Vela Plaža beach at Baška. West of Krk, Cres is a long, thin island of scanty pastures, dry stone walls and more sheep than people. The pine forests of the Tramuntana offer blissful walks and great birdwatching. South of Cres, and linked to it by a bridge, the island of Lošinj attracts tourists to the pretty town of Mali Lošinj. Between Lošinj and the mainland lies Rab, best known for Rab Town, a romantic medieval settlement built on a walled peninsula.

Planning your trip

Best time to visit Istria and Kvarner

Peak season in Isria and Kvarner runs July through August, when all the region's hotels, restaurants and other tourist facilities, such as water sports clubs, are up and running. Nightlife is buzzing, with various cultural events, and open-air bars and dance clubs. On the downside, beaches are crowded, and restaurants and bars so busy you may have to queue for a table. Accommodation prices rise steeply during this period, and availability may be scarce, so you should really book in advance.

Mid-season (May/June and September/October) is probably the most rewarding time to visit. Throughout June and September the sea is warm enough to swim (hardier types will also manage in May and October) and the beaches reasonably peaceful. Hotels and restaurants are open but not overly busy, so you'll get more personalized service. As temperatures are not unbearably hot, spring and autumn are also ideal periods for active land sports such as hiking and biking. An autumn visit to the region will certainly appeal to gourmets, as they'll catch seasonal delicacies such as truffles, mushrooms and chestnuts.

During low season, November to April, many hotels close down completely. Although you can't be guaranteed good weather, if you do visit during this period you can be almost certain there will be few foreigners around.

Getting to Istria and Kvarner

Air

From UK and Ireland **British Airways** flies to Dubrovnik from London Gatwick and to Zagreb from London Heathrow; **Croatian Airlines** flies to Zagreb from London Heathrow (with possible connecting flights to Dubrovnik, Pula, Split and Zadar); **EasyJet** flies to Dubrovnik from London Gatwick and Edinburgh and to Split from Bristol, London Gatwick or London Stansted; **Jet2.com** flies to Dubrovnik from Belfast, East Midlands, Edinburgh, Leeds Bradford, Manchester and Newcastle; to Pula from Glasgow, Leeds Bradford, Manchester and Newcastle; and to Split from Manchester; **Monarch** flies to Dubrovnik from Bristol, London Gatwick, Manchester; **Ryanair** flies to Zadar from Liverpool; **Thomsonfly** flies to Dubrovnik from London Gatwick and Manchester, and to Pula from Birmingham, London Gatwick and Manchester; and **Aer Lingus** flies to Dubrovnik from Dublin.

From rest of Europe There are direct flights to Croatia from most European capitals. Carriers include **Aeroflot**, **Air France/KLM**, **Austrian Airlines**, **Germanwings**, **Lufthansa**, **TAP Portugal** and **Turkish Airlines**.

From North America There are no direct flights from the US to Croatia.

Airport information Zagreb Airport (T01-456 2222, www.zagreb-airport.hr) has two banks, a post office, a duty-free shop, newsagents, a bar and restaurant, plus a number of rent-a-car companies, including **Hertz** (T01-456 2635, www.hertz.hr) and **HM Rentacar** (T01-370 4535, www.hm-rentacar.hr). Zagreb airport is 15 km south of the city centre.

Don't miss…

An airport bus, run by **Pleso** (T01-633 1999, www.plesoprijevoz.hr), makes regular runs between the airport and Zagreb Bus Station, a ticket costs 30Kn.

Pula Airport (T052-530 105, www.airport-pula.hr) has a duty-free shop and a bar, plus a number of rent-a-car companies, including **Avis** (T052-224 350, www.avis.com.hr) and **Hertz** (T052-210 868, www.hertz.hr). Pula airport is 7 km east of the city centre. An airport shuttle bus makes regular runs between the airport and the city centre, a ticket costs 15Kn.

Split Airport (T021-203555, www.split-airport.hr) has a bank, a post office, a duty-free shop, newsagents, and bar and restaurant, plus car-hire companies including **Hertz** (T021 895 230, www.hertz.hr) and **Uni Rent** (T021-895 223, www.uni-rent.net). Split airport is 25 km west of the city centre. An airport bus, run by **Pleso** (T021-203119, www.plesoprijevoz.hr), runs at regular intervals between the airport and Split's bus station (in the city centre, opposite the ferry port), a ticket costs 30Kn.

Dubrovnik Airport (T020-773100, www.airport-dubrovnik.hr) has a bank, a duty-free shop, a bar, plus car-hire companies including **Avis** (T020-773811, www.avis.com.hr) **Hertz** (T020-771 568, www.hertz.hr). Dubrovnik airport is 21 km southeast of the city centre. An airport bus, run by **Atlas** (T020-442222, www.atlas-croatia.com) makes regular runs between the airport and Dubrovnik Bus Station, passing the outer walls of the old town en route, a ticket costs 35Kn.

Rail
Regular daily international trains run direct to Zagreb from Venice, Ljubljana, Vienna, Budapest, Munich, Belgrade and Sarajevo.

The cheapest and fastest route from the UK is London–Paris–Venice–Zagreb, taking **Eurostar** (www.eurostar.com) through the Channel Tunnel. The entire journey takes about 39 hours and requires an overnight train. Prices vary greatly depending on how far in advance you book. For further details or information about alternative routes, contact **Rail Europe** (www.raileurope.co.uk), or check out the **Man in Seat Sixty-One** (www.seat61.com), an excellent website dedicated to travelling without flying.

If you are an EU passport holder and plan to travel across Europe to Croatia, consider buying a 'Global' **Inter Rail** (www.interrailnet.com) pass, offering unlimited second-class train travel in 30 countries. If you are 25 or under, a 15-day Global Inter Rail pass costs €307; if you are 26-59, it costs €435; and if you are 60 or over it costs €392.

Road

There are good road links to Croatia from the neighbouring countries of Slovenia, Hungary, Bosnia and Herzegovina, and Serbia and Montenegro. Visitors arriving from Italy or Austria will pass through Slovenia.

Eurolines (www.eurolines.co.uk) runs a network of long-distance buses all over Europe. Though there is no longer a direct bus from the UK to Croatia, the journey is possible with changes in France or Germany.

Sea

Croatia is well connected to Italy by overnight ferries the year through, and by additional fast daytime catamarans in summer. Although most of these services operate between Italy and Dalmatia, there are several lines running between Italy and Istria.

In high-season, it is possible to arrive in Istria by boat from Italy. **Venezia Lines** operates catamarans from Venice to Poreč and Rovinj, and Venice to Pula and Mali Lošinj. **Emilia Romagna Lines** runs catamarans from Ravenna to Rovinj, and from Rimini to Lošinj.

Ferry and catamaran company websites: Emilia Romagna Lines (www. emiliaromagnalines.it), **Venezia Lines** (www.venezialines.com).

Transport in Istria and Kvarner

Rail

All major Croatian cities, except Dubrovnik, are connected by rail. Train travel into more remote regions has been limited by topography, the rocky Dinaric Alps making it extremely difficult to build railways. Trains are operated by **Hrvatske Zeljeznice** (Croatian Railways, www.hznet.hr).

The most useful long-distance route for the regions of Istria and Kvarner is Zagreb–Rijeka (four hours) four trains daily. It is also possible to travel by train Rijeka-Pula (2½ hours) though this involves a change at Lupoglav. Arriving from Slovenia, there is a once-daily summer-only service Ljubljana-Pula (four hours).

The **InterRail Global pass** (www.interrailnet.com) provides train travel throughout Croatia and the other 29 participating European countries.

For national information contact **Zagreb Train Station**, T060-313333, www.hznet. hr. **Pula Train Station**, Kolodvorska 5, T052-541733. **Rijeka Train Station**, Krešmirova 5, T060-3334444.

Road

Bicycle Croatia is a great destination for mountain biking but be aware that locals drive fast and occasionally a little recklessly on major mainland roads and are not used to cyclists. The islands, however, are perfect for exploring by bicycle.

Bus/coach Buses tend to be slightly faster and marginally more expensive than trains, and they are generally less comfortable. However, while train services are limited, by using the bus you can get from any major city to the most remote village, albeit with a few changes en route. There are numerous private companies, each operating on their own terms, so there's no such thing as an unlimited travel pass. Prices and quality of buses vary greatly from company to company, and a return ticket is sometimes, but not always, cheaper than two one-way tickets.

For national information contact **Zagreb Bus Station**, T060-313333, www.akz.hr. **Rijeka Bus Station**, Trg Žabica 1, T060-302010, www.autotrans.hr. **Pula Bus Station**, Trg I. Istarske brigade bb, T060-304090. **Poreč Bus Station**, Rade Koncara 1, T052-432153. **Rovinj Bus Station**, Trg na lovki 6, T060-333111.

Car Having a car obviously makes you more independent, so you can plan your itinerary more freely. However, it also creates various problems that you would not encounter if using public transport. Medieval harbor towns such as Rovinj, and hilltowns such as Motovun and Grožnjan, are traffic free, so you'll have to park outside the walls – even then, finding a place can be difficult (and expensive) as the more central parking spots are reserved for residents with permits. Having a car can also make ferry transfers to the Kvarner islands extremely problematic: during high season be prepared to sit in queues to get a place on the boat (there is no reservation system for vehicles: you buy a ticket and then it's first come, first aboard).

Petrol stations are generally open daily 0700-1800, and often until 2200 in summer. The larger cities and major international roads have 24-hour petrol stations.

Hrvatski Autoklub (Croatian Automobile Club) T1987, hak.hr, offers a 24-hour breakdown service.

Car hire: Car hire is available at all the main airports. For one week in summer, expect to pay in the region of €387 for a small car such as a Fiat Seicento, or €505 for a Peugeot 208. Payments can be made by credit card, and your credit card number will be taken in lieu of a deposit. Most companies require drivers to be 21 or over.

Sea

The Croatian Adriatic has 48 inhabited islands, many of which can be reached by ferry. There are regular connections between the mainland ports of Rijeka, Zadar, Split and Dubrovnik to nearby islands.

Prices are reasonable as the state-owned ferry company **Jadrolinija** has been subsidized by the government in an attempt to slow down depopulation of islands. As well as connecting the islands, Jadrolinija operates a twice-weekly overnight coastal service (with cabins available) running from Rijeka to Dubrovnik, stopping at Split, Stari Grad (island of Hvar) and Korčula Town en route.

Sample high season prices are: Rijeka–Split by ferry, one way, passenger 164Kn, car 448Kn; Rijeka–Cres by catamaran, one way, passenger 45Kn; Rijeka–Rab Town by catamaran, one way, passenger 60Kn.

In addition to Jadrolinija, a number of smaller local companies run ferries and catamarans on certain routes. In the Kvarner region, **Linijska Nacionalna Plovidba** operates ferries from Valbiska (Krk) to Lopar (Rab), while **Rapska Plovidba** runs ferries Jablanac (mainland) to Mišnjak (Rab), and between Rab Town (Rab) and Lun (Pag).

Ferry and catamaran websites: **Jadrolinija** (jadrolinija.hr), **Linijska Nacionalna Plovidba** (lnp.hr), **Rapska Plovidba** (rapska-plovidba.hr).

Where to stay in Istria and Kvarner

Along the coast, private accommodation, either in a rented room or apartment, is the best choice in terms of cost, facilities and insight into the way the locals live. However, if you feel like splashing out and being pampered here and there, the hotels listed in this guide have been selected for their authentic atmosphere and central location. There aren't any websites listing private accommodation, but local tourist offices often have details and their websites are listed throughout the book.

Hotels

Croatian tourism dates back to the late 19th century when the region was under Austro-Hungary, and so along the coast you'll find a number of Vienna Secession-style hotels built for the Central European aristocracy of the time, the best examples being in Opatija.

During the tourist boom of the 1970s and 1980s, many of the older hotels were neglected in favour of large modern complexes, which sprang up in popular resorts such as Poreč and Rovinj. Although they tend to be vast and somewhat impersonal, these socialist-era hotels are equipped with excellent sports facilities, generally overlook the sea and are discreetly hidden by careful landscaping, a short walk from the centre of town. Over the last few years, some have been totally refurbished and have introduced chic minimalist design and wellness centres, bringing them into the luxury market.

The third and most recent breed of hotel are the small, private, family-run establishments, often in refurbished town houses, which have opened over the last decade and are now united under the **National Association of Small and Family Hotels**. For a full list, check out the website, www.omh.hr.

All hotels are officially graded by the Ministry of Tourism into five categories: five-star, luxury; four-star, de luxe; three-star, first class; two-star, moderate; and one-star, budget. Classified hotels are listed by the Croatian National Tourist Board (www.croatia.hr) under their respective regions.

When referring to price lists, you will find that some hotels list half board and full board only. Simple 'bed and breakfast' works out only very slightly cheaper than half board, but is recommended as, by and large, hotel restaurants lack atmosphere, and the standard of the food unfortunately reflects the savings made in order to be able to offer cheap package deals. You are far better off eating out in local restaurants.

Last but not least, if you are staying on the coast it is well worth asking for a room with a sea view (most of which have balconies); it may cost a little more, but makes all the difference when you wake up in the morning.

Private accommodation

Along the coast you will find a plethora of families offering *sobe* (rooms) and *apartmani* (apartments) for rent, usually with en suite bathrooms and simple self-catering facilities provided. These can be in anything from quaint, old stone cottages with gardens to modern concrete-block three-storey houses with spacious balconies. Hosts are generally welcoming and hospitable, and many visitors find a place they like and then return each summer. Local tourist offices and travel agents have lists of recognized establishments and can arrange bookings for you. In busy areas, you'll also find people waiting for travellers at the ferry ports and bus stations, and offering rooms by word of mouth, but in this case you're not guaranteed to find the best standards.

Price codes

Where to stay

€€€€ over €300   **€€€** €200-300

€€ €100-200   **€** under €100

Price codes refer to the cost of two people sharing a double room in high season.

Restaurants

€€€ over €40   **€€** €20-40   **€** under €20

Price codes refer to the cost of a two-course meal with a drink, including service and cover charge.

Prices vary enormously depending on location, season and facilities provided, but you can expect to pay anything from 150-250Kn per person per day for a double room with an en suite bathroom, and anything from 400-1200Kn per day for a four-person apartment with a kitchen and dining area. Note that there is normally a 30% surcharge for stays of less than three nights.

A British-based operator specializing in quality private villas and apartments for holiday rentals in top Croatian resorts is **Croatian Villas Ltd** (Wood Green Business Centre, 5 Clarendon Road, Wood Green, London N22 6XJ, T020-8888 6655, www.croatianvillas.com).

Agrotourism

An increasingly popular accommodation option is so-called agrotourism: farmhouses offering overnight accommodation and home cooking. This is a great solution for families with young children, as exploring the farm and getting to know the animals is guaranteed to go down well with kids. To date, the idea has only really taken off in Istria, but the potential throughout the country is enormous.

Most of these establishments are off the beaten track (you normally need a car to reach them) and offer bed and breakfast deals in simply furnished rooms with en suite bathrooms. Many also have a restaurant area, often done out in rustic style, serving authentic local dishes (generally far superior to the food served in commercial restaurants), along with their own wine, cheese and olive oil. Some of the larger centres also offer a range of sporting activities such as horse riding and mountain biking.

Prices vary greatly depending on the type of room, the location and season, but expect to pay anything from 180-320Kn per person per day for a double room (with an en suite bathroom) with breakfast in August.

For a list of farms and rural homes offering overnight accommodation and meals in Istria check out histrica.com/offer/agritourism.

Camping

The sunny, dry climate and unspoilt nature make Croatia an ideal place for camping. Of at least 130 registered campsites, about 90% are on the mainland coast or on the islands, many backed by pinewoods overlooking the sea. Most operate from early May to early October, are well run and offer basic facilities such as showers and toilets and a small bar, while the larger ones may include restaurants and extensive sports facilities, such as scuba-diving courses and mountain bike rentals. The most developed regions in terms of capacity and facilities provided are Istria and Kvarner. As in other European countries, camping outside of designated areas is prohibited.

Lighthouses

Another novel and highly popular form of accommodation is the lighthouse. Along the Croatian coast, there are now 11 carefully restored lighthouses with apartments to rent on a weekly basis. Nine of these are on islands (you will be taken there and brought back by boat), and three on peninsulas along the mainland coast. In Istria, these include Savudrija (Umag), Rt Zub (Novigrad), Sv Ivan (Rovinj) and Porer (Pula).

Most lighthouses have one or two apartments sleeping anything from two to eight people, and several are still home to a resident lighthouse keeper. However, you can be sure of extreme isolation and minimum contact with the outside world, as most of them are located on lonely islets far out to sea. Each apartment has electricity, running water, TV and a fully equipped kitchen.

Bed linen and blankets are provided, but be sure to take a week's provisions as there will be no chance of shopping once you are there, unless you come to a special arrangement with local fishermen or the lighthouse keeper.

Prices vary greatly depending on the size of the apartment, location and season, but as an indicator the cost of renting a four-person apartment in the lighthouse of Sv Ivan, near Rovinj, are as follows: July to August €129 per day; June and September €99 per day; and during the rest of the year €79 per day. However, as this has become a hugely popular alternative, be sure to book several months in advance.

For further details contact **Adriatica Net** ① *Heinzelova 62a, Zagreb, T01-241 5611, www.adriatica.net*, who have an online booking service.

For further information contact **Kamping Udruženje Hrvatske** (Croatian Camping Union, Pionirska 1, Poreč, T052-451324, www.camping.hr). Their excellent website lists all official campsites, complete with contact details, facilities and prices. Naturist campsites are also listed and marked 'FKK'.

Naturist camps

Naked bathing was first pioneered in Croatia in the early 20th century and Europe's first naturist campground opened here in 1953. Today there are 20 naturist campsites, almost all along the coast and on the islands, attracting visitors from Germany, Austria, the Netherlands, Italy and Slovenia, as well as other countries around the world. Europe's largest naturist camp, Koversada (dating from 1961), is in Istria, and can provide accommodation for up to 5000 visitors.

For more information about naturism in Croatia, including a list of naturist camps with comments from people who have stayed at them, check out the **Croatia Naturally** website, cronatur.com.

Youth hostels

There are now over 100 hostels dotted around the country, but only eleven are recognized by **Hostelling International** (HI, www.hihostels.com). Of these, only three are in Istria and Kvarner, and they are in Pula, Rijeka, and Veli Lošinj (on the island of Lošinj). The remaining hostels (not recognized by HI) range from friendly low-key establishments to noisy and chaotic party dens. Nonetheless, all provide basic but comfortable dormitory-style accommodation (expect to pay around 120-180Kn per person per night, depending on the time of year), and some offer the option of half or full board. For information about HI-recoginsed hostels, contact **Hrvatski Ferijalni i Hostelski Savez** (Croatian Youth Hostel Association, Savska 5/1, 10000 Zagreb, T01-482 9294, www.hfhs.hr).

Food and drink in Istria and Kvarner

Food

Croatian cuisine can be divided into two main groups: Mediterranean along the coast and Continental in the inland regions. That said, each region has its own particular specialities reflecting its geography, history and culture. Croatia's highly complex past is clearly evident in its cooking, which displays the traces left by centuries of occupation by three foreign empires: the Venetians brought pasta and risotto to the coast; Austro-Hungary introduced paprika-flavoured goulash and strudel inland; and the Ottoman Turks bequeathed the region with *sarma* (stuffed sauerkraut rolls) and baklava.

Compared with the rest of Croatia, in Istria you can expect slightly more adventurous dishes with extra care given to presentation, probably due to the Italian influence. Look out for the regional speciality, *tartufi* (truffles), usually served with pasta or steak, and risotto and pasta dishes *mare monti*, literally meaning 'sea and mountains', which combine shellfish and mushrooms. The best oysters and mussels are to be found in Limski Kanal, between Rovinj and Poreč. On the meat front, Istrians prepare delicious *srnetina* (venison) stew, normally served with *njoki* (gnocchi) or *fuži*, a local form of pasta. As in Dalmatia, rich casseroles can be prepared under a *peka* (a metal dome, which is placed over a terracotta pot and covered with white embers, for a slow cooking process), but in Istria it's known as a *cirepnja*. Regarding side dishes, you'll find delicious, colourful salads combining mixed leaves such as *rukola* (rocket) and radicchio.

Eating out

For a full blown lunch or dinner, visit a *restoran* (restaurant), where you can expect formal service and a menu including a wide range of Croatian dishes. Most restaurants are open 1200-1500 and 1900-2300, and many, especially along the coast, have a large terrace for open-air dining through the summer months. For a simpler meal, try a *gostionica*, a place you can also go just to drink. Service will be less formal, but you can often land some excellent home cooking, and they tend to stay open all day, Monday to Saturday 0800-2300. The terms *konoba* (in Dalmatia) and *klet* (in Zagorje) were originally associated with places for making and storing wine, but the names are now used by many rustic-style restaurants serving local specialities. Some open in the evenings only and may stay open for late-night drinking. Most towns have a pizzeria, and some serve excellent pizza, comparable to the best in Italy. A few also offer a choice of substantial salads and a limited selection of pasta dishes.

For something sweet, call at a *slastičarnica*. Many are run by Albanians (one of former Yugoslavia's ethnic minorities) and they offer eastern goodies such as baklava (see above), along with a selection of *sladoled* (ice creams). Most are open 0800-2000, and serve coffee, tea and fruit juices, but no alcohol.

If you are travelling in inland Istria, look out for agrotourism centres, where you can expect quality local produce such as home-made cheese and wine, as well as unusual seasonal specialities such as *šparoge* (wild asparagus) in spring, and *tartufi* (truffles) and *gljive* (mushrooms) in autumn.

Menu reader

blitva sa krumpirom Swiss chard and potatoes with garlic and olive oil, a side dish

brodet a hearty Dalmatian fish stew made with onions and tomatoes, and served with polenta

crni rižot black risotto, made from cuttlefish ink

dagnje mussels

friganje lignje fried squid

Hvarska gregada a type of brodet made on the island of Hvar, using fish, onions, potatoes and fresh herbs, but no tomato

janjetina roast lamb, normally roast whole on a spit

kobasice sausages

kućice clams

mješanja salata mixed salad, usually lettuce, cucumber and tomato

na buzaru cooked with garlic, white wine and parsley to produce a delicious rich sauce

ostrige oysters

palačinke pancakes

paški sir a hard, salty sheep's cheese from the island of Pag

pašticada s njokima beef stewed in sweet wine and served with gnocchi

peka an ancient method of slow-cooking food (generally lamb, veal or octopus) when a terracotta pot is placed over white embers and covered by a metal dome; note that most restaurants require you to order peka dishes at least one day in advance

pršut smoked dried ham similar to Italian prosciutto

ražnjiči kebabs

riba na žaru barbecued fish, normally drizzled with olive oil and served with a wedge of lemon

rižot frutti di mare seafood risotto, normally combining mussels, clams and prawns

rižot sa škampima shrimp risotto, invariably served with a splash of cream at the end

salata od hobotnice octopus salad, made from octopus, boiled potatoes, onion and parsley, dressed with olive oil and vinegar

rožata a Dubrovnik speciality, similar to crème caramel

škampi shrimps

škampi na buzaru shrimps cooked in garlic, white wine and parsley to produce a delicious rich sauce

sladoled ice cream

Eating in

If you opt for private accommodation you will probably have self-catering facilities. All cooking utensils and kitchen equipment such as pans, bowls, plates, glasses, cups and cutlery will be provided: if anything is missing ask your host and they will give you anything extra you require. Occasionally basics such as sugar, salt and pepper are provided – normally left by the people who were there before you.

You will probably also be supplied with a *džezver* – a metal coffee pot with a handle, used for preparing Turkish-style coffee, which is usually drunk here rather than instant, filter or espresso coffee. Vacuum-packed ground coffee can be bought in general stores.

Drink

Coffee and tea Meeting friends for *kava* (coffee) is something of a morning ritual. Many bars open as early as 0600, and are busy all day. While most people prepare Turkish coffee at home, cafés and bars serve Italian-style espresso and cappuccino. If you ask for *čaj* (tea) you will be given *šipak* (rosehip) served with lemon; if you want English-style tea ask for *indijski čaj sa mlijekom* (Indian tea with milk). Most cafés have tables outside, even in winter, and there is no extra charge for sitting down.

Wine Croatian wines are little known abroad as they are exported in relatively small quantities, though some of them, such as the highly esteemed Dingač, are excellent. By and large the north produces whites and the south reds, though there are some exceptions.

Among the whites, names to look out for are: Pošip and Grk (from the island of Korčula), Vugava (island of Vis), Žlahtina (island of Krk), Malvazija (Istria), Graševina and Traminac (Slavonia). Of the reds, be sure to try: Dingač (Pelješac Peninsula), Plavac (islands of Hvar and Vis), Babič (Primošten) and Teran (Istria).

To buy top wines at better prices, go direct to the producer. In Istria, the regional tourist board has drawn up a series of wine routes with a list of producers who receive visitors, for a map check out the website, istra.com/vino.

Lower-grade wines are bottled in one-litre bottles with a metal cap, while better wines come in 0.75 litre bottles with a cork. Sometimes you will find the same label on both, but the 0.75-litre bottle will be more expensive and of higher quality. Most bars serve wine by the glass, either by the *dec* (1 dl) or *dva deca* (2 dl).

Beer Beer was introduced to Croatia under Austro-Hungary, when the Hapsburgs built the first breweries to supply their soldiers. Light-coloured lager, served well chilled, is the most common sort of beer, with popular brands being Karlovačko, Kaltenburg, Laško Zlatorog and Ožujsko. Tomislav is a stout (dark beer) brewed in Zagreb. When you buy beer by the bottle, you pay a small deposit, which you can get back upon return of the empties and display of the receipt. Imported draught Guinness is popular but tends to be about three times the price of local beer.

Spirits *Rakija*, a distilled spirit usually made from a grape base, was introduced to the region by the Turks, and is normally drunk as an aperitif before eating, but can also be taken as a digestive at the end of a meal. The most popular types are: *loza* (made from grapes), *travarica* (flavoured with aromatic grasses), *šljivovica* (made from plums) and *pelinkovac* (flavoured with juniper berries and bitter herbs, similar to Italian amaro). In addition, there are various regional specialities, such as biska (flavoured with mistletoe) in inland Istria. Imported spirits such as whisky and gin are popular but expensive.

Festivals in Istria and Kvarner

January

Nova Godina (1 Jan) Croats celebrate the arrival of New Year with open-air concerts and fireworks in all the big cities: in Rijeka they gather on the Korzo.

February

Karneval (around Shrove Tue) In the days leading up to Lent, many towns and villages in Croatia celebrate carnival. The biggest celebrations take place in Rijeka (www.rijecki-karneval.hr). The main event is the **International Carnival Parade**, held on the Sun before Shrove Tuesday and attracting over 100,000 spectators and several thousand participants in costumes and masks. Young men dress up as zvončari (clothed in a sheepskin cape, a grotesque animal mask with horns, and a large iron bell tied around the waist). Traditionally, their role is to chase away the forces of evil and invite the coming of spring and new life.

April

Dani Šparoga The Asparagus Festival in Lovran, near Rijeka, is one of several food festivals staged here, with a dozen or so of the town's restaurants preparing dishes made from local seasonal delicacy. The event closes with the making of a giant omelette.

May

Theatre Festival Rijeka (early May; www.theatrefestival-rijeka.hr) 1-week European theatre festival staged in Rijeka.

June

Fiumanka (mid-Jun; www.fiumanka.eu) 4-day sailing regatta from Rijeka to Omišalj (on the island of krk) and back.
Pula Superiorum (mid-Jun; www.pula superiorum.com) Celebrates Pula's Roman origins with 3 days of re-enactments.
Rijeka Summer Nights (mid-Jun to late Jul; www.rijeckeljetnenoci.com) Open-air theatre and concerts in Rijeka's old town.

Dani Trešanja In Lovran, the Cherry Festival sees these tasty little red fruits consumed in large quantities in local restaurant and cafes. The festival closes with the sampling of a 5-m cherry strudel.

July and August

Hartera Festival (mid-Jul; www.hartera.com) This 3-day rock, indie-electro and dance music festival is held in a former-paper factory in Rijeka. The 2012 event saw the London-based Asian Dub Foundation Sound System and the Norwegian electronic band GusGus performing.
Jazz is Back (mid-Jul; www.jazzisbackbp.com) 3-week jazz festival held in the medieval hilltown of Grožnjan.
Motovun Film Festival (late Jul; www.motovunfilmfestival.com) This 5-day international festival of avant-garde cinema, founded in 1999, takes place in the medieval hilltown of Motovun.
Osor Music Evenings (late Jul to late Aug; www.osorskveceri.org) Classic music recitals in the village of Osor on Cres.
Pula Festival Igranog Filma (late Jul; www.pulafilmfestival.hr) The Pula Film Festival is a 2-week competitive event held in Pula's Roman Arena and at Kaštel. It features films from both Croatia and abroad.
Rapska Fjera (late Jul) Rab Tournament is a 3-day event held in Rab Town to record the defence of the town by knights with crossbows in 1364. Locals dress in medieval costume, streets are lit by torches, there's music and demonstrations of traditional skills such as coin minting, grape treading and flour milling.
Seasplash Reggae Festival (late Jul; www.seasplash.net) This 4-day reggae festival is held at Fort Punta Christo, Štinjan, near Pula.
Koncerti u Eufraziani (Jul and Aug; www.concertsinbazilika.com) In Poreč, sacral and secular music concerts are held in the Basilica of St Euphrasius.

Jazz u Lapidarju (Jul and Aug; www.jazz inlap.com) Jazz in Lapidarium is a jazz festival held in the courtyard of Poreč Town Museum, attracting classical and contemporary performers.

Grisia (early Aug) Held in Rovinj's old town, this is a vast open-air art exhibition.

outlook Festival (late Aug; www.outlook festival.com) This 4-day dubstep festival is held at Fort Punta Christo, Štinjan, near Pula.

___

September

Dolphin of Poreč (early Sep; www.poreck delfin.com) 2-day swimming festival in Poreč, including marathon and sprint races.

Dimensions Festival (early Sep; www.dimensionsfestival.com) This 4-day electronic festival is held at Fort Punta Christo, Štinjan, near Pula.

TeTa (late Sep) 1-day festival Terana & Tartufa (Teran red wine and truffles) held on the main square in motovun.

Marunada (late Sep to early Oct) The chestnut festival is held in Lovran, with local eateries and cafes serving cakes and sweets.

___

October and November

Truffle festivals held at various locations in Inland Istria, with the biggest events taking place in the villages of Livade and Buzet.

___

December

Christmas celebrations throughout the region.

Essentials A-Z

Accident and emergency
In the case of an emergency requiring police attention, dial 192. For an ambulance, dial 94.

Electricity
Croatia functions on 220 volts AC, 50Hz; plugs have 2 round pins (as in most of continental Europe).

Health
Most EU countries have a reciprocal healthcare agreement with Croatia, meaning that you pay a basic minimum for a consultation and hospital treatment is free if you can show your European Health Insurance Card (EHIC).

For minor complaints visit a *ljekarna* (pharmacy), recognized by its green cross outside; most are open Mon-Fri 0800-1900 and Sat 0800-1400, and in larger cities at least one will be open 24 hrs. In an emergency, go to *hitno pomoč* (casualty). Dial 94 for an ambulance.

Language
Croatian belongs to the South Slavic branch of the Slavic group of languages – a similar language is spoken by Serbs, Montenegrins and Bosnians. Most people working in tourism, as well as the majority of younger Croatians, speak good English, so you won't have much of a problem communicating unless you get off the beaten track. If you do make the effort to learn a few words and phrases, though, your efforts are likely to be rewarded with a smile of appreciation.

Money
The official currency is the kuna (Kn), which is divided into 100 lipa. It is now possible to buy kune outside Croatia, though you may have to order them from your bank several days in advance, as there is a relatively low demand for the currency. Although Croatia is scheduled to join the EU in Jul 2013, it will not adopt the euro immediately.

In the meantime, the euro is the most readily accepted foreign currency. Most towns and villages, even on the islands, have a *banka* (bank), generally open Mon-Fri 0700-1900 and Sat 0700-1300, and most have an ATM too. Major credit cards (**American Express**, **Diners Club**, **MasterCard** and **Visa**) are widely accepted.

Safety
Despite the negative image created by the war, Croatia has a lower crime rate than most other European countries. Rare cases of violent crime are usually targeted at specific persons connected to organized crime. Foreigners do not appear to be singled out.

Although military action connected to the war ended in 1995, the problem of landmines, mostly along the former front lines in eastern Slavonia and the Krajina, remains. De-mining is not complete: if you are passing through such areas, exercise caution and do not stray from known safe roads and paths.

Time
GMT +1.

Tipping
Tips are not included on bills. At the end of a good meal at a restaurant it is customary to leave 10% extra if you are satisfied with the service. Bar staff do not expect tips.

Tourist information
The **Croatian National Tourist Board**, croatia.hr, covers the whole country.

Visas

EU citizens do not need a visa but do require a passport to enter Croatia for stays of up to 90 days. Once Croatia joins the EU in Jul 2013, the usual EU regulations will apply regarding longer stays. For further details, visit the **Croatian Ministry of Foreign Affairs** website, www.mvp.hr.

Contents

Footprint features

Istria

Pula

Pula is something of an enigma. Here, magnificent ancient Roman ruins stand side by side with a declining industrial port, in a city that is Istria's administrative and economic centre. As the historic attractions in the city centre (notably the monumental first-century Roman amphitheatre, known as the 'Arena') can be explored in just one day, most visitors prefer to base themselves in nearby Rovinj, which is infinitely prettier and more restful, then do Pula as a day-trip. However, with two well-equipped marinas, the ACI marina directly in front of the city centre and Veruda marina 4 km south of the centre, Pula is a popular destination for yachters, as well as holidaymakers on package deals, who normally sleep in the large resort hotels on the coast at Verudela and Medulin. Also close to Pula lies Brijuni National Park, well worth a day-trip in itself.

Arriving in Pula

Getting there Pula Airport (T052-530105, www.airport-pula.hr) is 7 km east of the city centre and is served by shuttle bus (15Kn). The bus station is at Trg I. Istarske brigade bb, T060-304090. For regional bus travel, see page 8. **Venezia Lines**, venezialines. com, operate a catamaran from Pula to Venice, April to October. The train station is at Kolodvorska 5, T052-541733. For regional train travel, see page 8.

Tourist information Pula city tourist office is at Forum 3, T052-219197, www.pulainfo.hr.

Arena

ⓘ *Flavijevska ulica, T052-219028, May-Sep daily 0800-2100, Oct-Apr daily 0900-1700, 40Kn.*
Pula's top sight has to be this beautifully preserved first-century Roman amphitheatre. Designed to host gladiator fights and able to accommodate 22,000 spectators, way beyond the city population of that time, it is the sixth-largest building of its type in the world (after the Colosseum in Rome, and the amphitheatres in Verona, Catania, Capua and Arles). The outer walls are remarkably intact, though through the centuries stones from the inside have been carried off for use on other buildings. Originally the interior would have been encircled by tiers of stone seats, the central floor would have been covered with sand, and a velarium (large awning) would have been used as a temporary roof structure, to shelter spectators from the sun and rain.

The Arena fell into disuse in the sixth century, when gladiator games were forbidden. During the 16th century the Venetians planned to transfer it, stone by stone, to Venice, though fortunately a local senator, Gabriele Emo, protested and the project was abandoned. The building was restored in the early 19th century by General Marmont under Napoleon's Illyrian provinces.

Each summer, the Arena hosts open-air concerts, with recent performers including Elton John and Manu Chao, as well as the annual Pula Film Festival (see Festivals, page 16).

Rimski Forum

ⓘ *Forum bb.*
This vast, paved piazza has been the city's most important public meeting space since Roman times. It's closed to traffic and overlooked by popular open-air cafés, the Renaissance Town Hall, the city tourist office and the Temple of Augustus (see below).

Pula

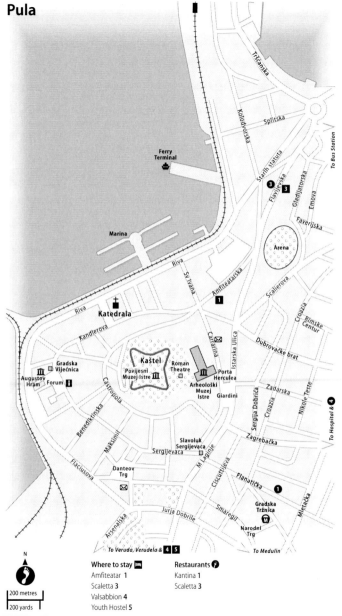

Where to stay 🛏
Amfiteatar **1**
Scaletta **3**
Valsabbion **4**
Youth Hostel **5**

Restaurants 🍴
Kantina **1**
Scaletta **3**

N

200 metres
200 yards

Augustov Hram

ⓘ *Forum bb, Jun-Sep Fri-Mon 0900-2200, Sat-Sun 0900-1500, May and Oct 0900-2100, Nov-Apr by appointment, 10Kn.*

On the north side of the Forum square, the well-preserved Roman Temple of Augustus has an open portico supported by six tall columns with Corinthian capitals. It was built in the early first century AD to celebrate the cult of Augustus, who founded the Roman Empire in 27 BC. Under Byzantine rule it was converted into a church and later used as a granary. Today it houses a lapidarium, displaying pieces of Roman sculpture.

Slavoluk Sergijevaca

ⓘ *Ulica Sergijevaca.*

The Triumphal Arch of the Sergi was built in the first century BC to honour the local Sergi family for their role at the Battle of Actium, fought between the Roman fleet of Octavian and the Roman-Egyptian fleet of Mark Antony and Cleopatra in 31 BC. The Sergis were on the side of Octavian, who was victorious and consequently went on to become the first Roman emperor under the name of Augustus.

Next to the arch stands the house where the Irish author James Joyce (1882-1941) lived briefly during a spell in Istria in 1905 – you can't miss it, there's a bronze sculpture of the man himself sitting on a bench out front.

West of the arch, Ulica Sergijevaca was the city's main street in Roman times and is now a pedestrian area lined with Pula's highest concentration of clothes shops.

Kaštel

For an impressive panorama over the city, follow Castropola street up to the hilltop Kaštel. The present fortress was built by the Venetians in 1630 and later renovated by the Austrians in 1840. It now houses the **Historical Museum of Istria** ⓘ *T052-211566, www.pmi.hr, Apr-Sep daily 0800-2100, Oct-Mar daily 0900-1700, 10Kn*. However, for most the city views are more rewarding than the museum itself. In summer, the central courtyard at the Kaštel is used for open-air cultural events including the Pula Film Festival.

Gradska Tržnica

ⓘ *Narodni Trg, Mon-Sat 0700-1330, Sun 0700-1200.*

Built as a covered market in 1903, this iron-and-glass structure was revolutionary in its time. The daily fish and meat market is still held inside, while fruit and vegetable stands are set up outside, in the shade of a fine row of chestnut trees.

Brijuni National Park

ⓘ *The national park office is in the mainland village of Fažana (10 km northwest of Pula), opposite the ferry quay, T052-525888, www.brijuni.hr.*

The only way to visit the national park is as part of an organized group and reservations should be made several days in advance. Tickets cost 125-210Kn (depending on the time of year), which includes the boat ride and a tour of the grounds conducted by a professional guide. National park boats leave from Fažana and ferry visitors back and forth to the largest island, Veli Brijuni. It is possible to stay overnight (see Where to stay, page 31).

Alternatively several tour companies offer full-day excursions to Brijuni by boat from Pula, with lunch included, but this works out more costly and is very touristy.

Having remained uninhabitable through the centuries due an infestation of malaria-carrying mosquitoes, in 1893 Brijuni was bought by Paul Kupelweiser, an Austrian industrial magnate. Kupelweiser employed the German scientist Robert Koch (founder of modern medical bacteriology, 1843-1910) to purge the place of the disease. Kupelweiser then set about creating a prestigious health resort: he laid out the parkland, tree-lined avenues and exotic planting, had fresh water and electricity brought to the island and built a heated seawater swimming pool. Brijuni fast became a haven for Vienna's nobility and high society, with elite guests including Archduke Franz Ferdinand and the German writer Thomas Mann. In the 1920s, under Italian rule, a casino, polo club and tennis courts were built.

Then, after the Second World War, it became President Tito's official summer residence. He entertained countless world leaders here, as well as glamorous friends such as Richard Burton and Elizabeth Taylor.

After he died, the Brijuni archipelago, made up of 14 islands and islets, was made a national park, and the largest island, Veli Brijun, opened to the public. This low-lying island, with its beautifully tended parkland, herds of deer and strutting peacocks, makes a good day trip from Pula.

Here, visitors can see the safari park, with zebras, antelopes, llamas and elephants, many of which were given to Tito as presents from world leaders. It is a lovely place to walk, but other options are to rent a bike or an electric buggy.

There's also a museum housing a photography exhibition *Tito on Brijuni* showing the great man enjoying his summer retreat with friends and colleagues.

Rovinj and around

On Istria's west coast, 35 km northwest of Pula, Rovinj is composed of densely packed medieval town houses, built into a hillside and crowned by a church and elegant bell tower. Down below, Venetian-style coloured façades curve their way around a pretty fishing harbour, rimmed with open-air cafés, restaurants and ice cream parlours. Out to sea lie a scattering of 14 small islands, while south of town, the green expanse of Zlatni Rt Park has tree-lined avenues and an indented shoreline with several pebble coves for bathing. The town's beauty and relaxed atmosphere have long made it popular with Croatian and Italian artists, writers, musicians and actors, and most visitors would vote it their favourite place to stay on the Istrian coast.

Arriving in Rovinj
Getting there The bus station is at Trg na Lokvi 6, T060-333111. Venezia Lines, venezialines.com, operate a catamaran from Rovinj to Venice (Italy), April to October. Emilia Romagna Lines, emiliaromagnalines.it, run a catamaran between Rovinj and Cesenatico and Ravenna (Italy), late June to early September.

Tourist information Rovinj city tourist office is at Obala P Budicina 12, T052-811566, www.tzgrovinj.hr.

Sv Eufemija
ⓘ *T052-815615, May-Oct daily 1000-1800, Nov-Apr on request, church free, bell tower 15Kn.*
From the harbour, a labyrinth of steep, narrow cobbled streets run up to the hilltop Church of St Euphemia. The building gained its baroque appearance in 1736, though there had been a church here for centuries. The 61-m Venetian bell tower, topped by a gleaming

bronze weather vane of St Euphemia, was erected in 1677. Euphemia, who lived in the region that is now northwest Turkey, was thrown to the lions in AD 304, during one of Emperor Diocletian's anti-Christian purges. According to legend, her remains were placed in a sixth-century marble sarcophagus, which floated out to sea from Constantinople and was washed ashore in Rovinj in AD 800. The sarcophagus in question is now kept within the church, covered by a finely embroidered gold cloth.

Kuča Batana
ⓘ *Obala Pina Budicina 2, T052-812593, www.batana.org, Jun-Sep daily 1000-1500, 1800-2200; Oct-Dec and Mar-May Tue-Sun 1000-1300, 1500-1700, 10Kn.*
On the seafront promenade, overlooking the harbour, the eco-museum 'Batana House' is named after the *batana*, a traditional local fishing boat. Telling the story of Rovinj's centuries-old fishing community, it occupies two floors of a 17th-century building.

Akvarij
ⓘ *Obala G Paliage 5, T052-804712, summer daily 0900-2100, winter by appointment, 15Kn.*
Dating back to 1891, Rovinj's aquarium is one of the oldest in Europe. Marine species such as octopuses, poisonous scorpion fish and large turtles are on display, plus other underwater creatures such as sponges and sea anemones.

Beaches
A short walk southeast of the old town, Zlatni Rt is a vast expanse of parkland planted with avenues of holm oaks, alpine pines, cedar and cypresses, and criss-crossed by footpaths leading down to a series of pebble coves ideal for bathing.

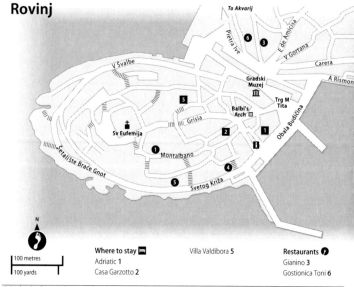

Rovinj

Where to stay 🛏
Adriatic 1
Casa Garzotto 2
Villa Valdibora 5

Restaurants 🍴
Gianino 3
Gostionica Toni 6

Other places for a dip are the nearby islets of Sv Katarina (St Catherine) and Crveni Otok (Red Island), both of which have pleasant rocky coastlines offering easy access to the water. In peak season, boats from the harbour leave every 30 minutes.

Limski Kanal
ⓘ *4 km north of Rovinj.*

Accessible by boat, the Lim Fjord is a 12-km-long flooded canyon, edged in part by dramatic limestone cliffs rising 120 m above the water, and in part by green slopes covered with woods of holm oak, ash and pines. Underwater springs give the seawater a low salt content, making it ideal for farming oysters and mussels, and several excellent fish restaurants have opened here, taking advantage of both the locally produced oysters and mussels and the spectacular setting. Various agencies offer day trips to Lim Fjord by boat, and depart from Rovinj harbour.

Poreč

Poreč, 45 km northwest of Pula, is Istria's most-visited seaside resort. The old town is quite tiny, a cluster of Venetian-style terracotta-roofed houses lying compact on a small peninsula. Founded as a Roman castrum (military camp) in the second century BC, the layout of the old town still follows the original Roman plan, though most of the present buildings date from between the 13th and 18th centuries. Here, Poreč's top attraction, the sixth-century Euphrasius Basilica, is decorated with golden Byzantine mosaics so stunning to have earned it a place on the UNESCO list of World Heritage Sites.

Café life centres on the seafront promenade overlooking the harbour, which is filled with fishing boats and water taxis that shuttle holidaymakers back and forth to beaches on the nearby islet of Sv Nikola (St Nicholas). South of the centre, Plava Laguna and Zelena Laguna make up a 6-km stretch of modern hotel complexes, cleverly hidden by landscaping and dense pinewoods.

A Miloša
G. Mazzinia
Carera
G Carduccia
M Benussia
Trg na Lokvi
J Rakovca
R Daveggia
N Quarantottia
Obala Vladimira Nazora
Obala Alda Negrija
To Zlatni Rt

Monte **1**
Puntalina **5**
Veli Jože **4**

Arriving in Poreč
Getting there The bus station is at Rade Končara 1, a five-minute walk from the old town, T052-432153. Venezia Lines, venezialines.com, operate a catamaran from Poreč to Venice, April-October.

Tourist information Poreč city tourist office at Zagrebačka 9, T052-451293, www.to-porec.com. The Istria regional tourist office is also in Poreč at Pionirksa 1, T051-452797, www.istra.com.

Decumanus
Laid out by the Romans in the first century BC, Decumanus is a wide, paved street that still forms the main thoroughfare through

the old town, running the length of the peninsula to Trg Marafor. Today it's lined with fine Romanesque and Gothic townhouses, several of which have been converted into boutiques and cafés at street level.

Eufrazijeva Basilica

ⓘ *Eufrazijeva bb, daily 0900-1800, 30Kn.*

Halfway down Decumanus, a narrow side street leads to Euphrasius Basilica, a well-signed complex consisting of a magnificent sixth-century basilica, a delightful atrium, an octagonal baptistery, a 16th-century bell tower and the bishop's palace. The interior of the church is decorated with glistening golden mosaics above, behind and around the main apse, making it one of the most important Byzantine monuments on the Adriatic, comparable to San Vitale in Ravenna. Above the altar, the central mosaic depicts the Virgin and Child, with the first Bishop of Poreč, St Mauro, to their right, and Bishop Euphrasius, who was responsible for the mosaic project, on their left. In front of the apse stands a 13th-century ciborium supported by four marble columns.

Trg Marafor

On the tip of the peninsula, Trg Marafor was once the site of a small Roman forum. The ruins of two Roman temples, dedicated to Mars and Neptune, can still be seen today.

Beaches

The best beaches are on Otok Sv Nikola (St Nicholas' Island). The island can be reached by regular taxi boats, which leave the harbour every half an hour through peak season.

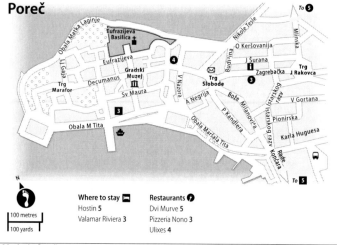

Poreč

100 metres
100 yards

Where to stay 🛏
Hostin **5**
Valamar Riviera **3**

Restaurants 🍴
Dvi Murve **5**
Pizzeria Nono **3**
Ulixes **4**

Truffles

The truffle is a subterranean European fungus, generally found in damp soils on or near the roots of oak trees. It can be white, brown or black, and although it grows approximately 30 cm below the soil, its scent is so strong that dogs and pigs can be trained to detect it. Fetching prices of up to €3000 per kg, the truffle is among the most expensive foodstuffs in the world: it is used in foie gras, and can also be eaten grated on pasta or steak, or made into a rich creamy sauce. Undoubtedly an acquired taste, past aficionados include Winston Churchill and Marilyn Monroe.

In Istria, about 500 registered truffle-hunters have a legal right to dig for this gnarled, tuberous fungus. However, each year between October and December an estimated 3000 people and three times as many dogs (usually a cross between a retriever and a hound) wander through Istria's forests and meadows searching for this prestigious delicacy, making it one of region's top sources of income and one of the main reasons why many people come here.

The largest truffle in the world, listed in the Guinness Book of Records, was unearthed in the Mirna Valley, Istria, on 2 November 1999. It was found by Giancarlo Zigante and his dog Diana, weighed 1.31 kg and measured 19.5 cm x 12.4 cm x 13.5 cm. Zigante decided not to sell it but instead prepared a dinner for 100 guests, and had the original cast in bronze. He now runs Zigante Tartufi, a small chain of shops specialiing in truffles and truffle-based products (see Shopping, page 36).

Inland Istria

Frequently overlooked by tourists but much loved by Croatians, inland Istria is sometimes compared to Tuscany, thanks to its undulating green landscapes and medieval, walled hill towns. This is the country's top area for agrotoursim (farms offering meals and overnight accommodation) and is at it prettiest in spring or autumn.

Many rural villages lie semi-abandoned, though it's fast becoming fashionable to have a restored stone holiday cottage in the area. The romantic fortified hilltop towns of Motovun and Grožnjan have established themselves as alternative cultural centres, the former with an annual festival of avant-garde film, the latter with its community of artists and craftsmen, plus an annual music summer school. The surrounding villages are much prized for rustic eateries serving dishes with truffles found locally in the Mirna Valley, along with Teran red wine, also from the area.

Motovun

ⓘ T052-681726, www.tz-motovun.hr, 25 km northeast of Poreč, there is no bus station at Motovun, private transport is recommended, Motovun tourist office is at Trg Andrea Antico 1.
This beautifully preserved fortified hill town is frequently included on tours of inland Istria as a model example of local architecture. There are no outstanding buildings, but the complex as a whole is exceptionally pretty, with medieval stone houses and a Venetian loggia surrounded by defensive walls, towers and town gates. In fact, due to its remarkable beauty, Motovun is on the UNESCO 'Tentative List' for World Heritage status. It is possible to walk a complete circuit of the ramparts, offering sweeping views of the oak forests and vineyards of the Mirna Valley – an area also renowned for its truffles.

Glagolitic script

Invented by Saint Cyril (AD 827-869) from Thessaloniki (Greece), the glagolitic script was the forerunner to Cyrillic, today used in Russia, Serbia and Montenegro, Bulgaria and Ukraine.

Cyril devised the 38-letter glagolitic alphabet (based on Greek characters) upon the request of the Moravian leader to the Byzantine Emperor, who wanted a form of writing that would more closely represent the sounds of the Slavic languages. Cyril and his brother, Saint Methodius (AD 826-884), then proceeded to translate books of the New Testament and develop a Slavonic liturgy, earning themselves the title of the 'Apostles of the Slavs'.

The script was used in many churches along the Croatian Adriatic coast right up until the 19th century, though it met resistance from certain members of the clergy who favoured Latin as a way of forging closer ties with Rome. However, Croatian secular literature was traditionally written in Latin script, as the majority of the elite were educated at universities in Italy or Austro-Hungary.

Each summer in late July, the informal Motovun Film Festival, www.motovunfilmfestival.com, takes place here – it's tremendously popular and is one of Croatia's most enjoyable cultural events; more than 70 films are shown in five venues, attracting 40,000 cinema buffs from all over Europe, see page 36.

Grožnjan

① *T052-776131, www.tz-groznjan.hr, 26 km northeast of Poreč, there is no bus station at Grožnjan, private transport is recommended, OK-Grožnjan tourist office is at Umberta Gorjana 3.*
This charming medieval hill town was all but abandoned until the mid-1960s, when it was rediscovered by painters, potters and sculptors, and proclaimed a 'Town of Artists'. They restored the crumbling medieval buildings, converting them into studios, workshops and galleries. Today it's a truly lovely place to visit, with partly preserved 14th-century town walls hugging a warren of narrow winding cobbled streets and old stone cottages, and at least 30 small art galleries.

Look out for the Venetian loggia adjoining the town gate, the baroque Church of Saints Mary, Vitus and Modest with a free-standing bell tower on the main square, and the tiny 16th-century Chapel of Saints Cosmas and Damian, decorated with frescoes by Ivan Lovrenčić in 1990, in front of the town gate. There are some well-marked footpaths leading to the surrounding villages, which make good walks.

Each year from May to October, Jeunesses Musicales Croatia, an international federation of young musicians, meets here for a summer school run by well-known international music professors.

And in July, the old streets are filled with the sounds of brass, woodwind and stringed instruments of varying tones and pitches, as musicians prepare for open-air evening as part of the 'Jazz is Back' festival (see Festivals, page 36).

Aleja Glagoljaša

① *Running for 7 km between Roč and Hum.*
The Glagolitic Alley was built in 1977 to record the historic importance of the Glagolitic script in this region. The route is marked by 11 monuments celebrating important events and people associated with this all-but-forgotten form of writing (see box, page 30). It ends in

Hum, which claims to be the smallest town in the world (population 17), and is made up of a dozen or so old stone houses and a tiny 12th-century Romanesque church. Most people come here specifically to eat at the renowned Humska Konoba (see Restaurants, page 35).

The monuments In Roč, at the junction for Hum, you can see the Pillar of the Čakav Parliament, a reference to Croatian self-rule and the Čakav dialect (one of three variants of the Croatian language). The second monument shows the Three-legged Table before Two Cypresses, with the trees symbolizing the apostles of the Slavs, St Cyril and St Methodius. Monument three is dedicated to the Assembly of Kliment of Ohrid – Kliment was a pupil of Cyril and Methodius, and he founded the first Slav university near Lake Ohrid.

The fourth monument, in front of the village church in Brnobici, is a lapidarium displaying Glagolitic inscriptions from various regions of former Yugoslavia, while monument five portrays Mount Učka partly hidden by clouds – in the Middle Ages it was regarded as the Croatian equivalent of Mount Olympus in Greece.

Istria listings

For hotel and restaurant price codes and other relevant information, see pages 10-15.

Where to stay

Pula *p22, map p23*

€€ Amfiteatar Hotel, Amfiteatarska 6, T052-375600, www.hotelamfiteatar.com. Ideally located just a 3-min walk from the Roman amphitheatre, this comfortable hotel offers 18 rooms with modern minimalist decor. There's a ground floor restaurant serving creative Mediterranean cuisine, with outdoor tables through summer. It opened in 2011, so everything is still relatively new and fresh.

€€ Ribarska Kolidba, Verudela 3, T052-391555, www.ribarskakolidba.com. Overlooking the marina, 3 km from Pula city centre, this small complex offers 19 modern apartments, sleeping 2-6, all with self-catering facilities and most with either a balcony or patio. Shared facilities include a heated outdoor pool, a lounge-bar and a restaurant with a sea-view terrace.

€€ Valsabbion, Pješčana uvala IX/26, T052-218033, www.valsabbion.hr. Overlooking the sea in Medulin, 4 km from the centre of Pula, this small luxury hotel has 10 cheerful guest rooms adorned with pine

furniture and primary coloured fabrics, plus fresh fruit and flowers. There's a swimming pool and gym on the top floor, and they offer beauty programmes such as facials, peeling and lazer treatments, plus massage. Note the once highly regarded restaurant has closed, though they still do a generous buffet breakfast.

€ Hotel Scaletta, Flavijevska 26, T052-541025, www.hotel-scaletta.com. Close to the Roman amphitheatre, this 12-room family-run hotel occupies a tastefully refurbished old town house. Rooms are decorated in sunny shades of ochre and green, and come with spanking new bathrooms. There's also an excellent restaurant with a summer terrace.

Brijuni National Park *p24*

€€€ Hotel Neptun-Istra, T052-525807, www.brijuni.hr. Overlooking the harbour on the island of Veli Brijuni, this big, 1970s-style hotel has 67 rooms and 20 suites, the latter with terraces and sea views. Guests can leave their cars in the guarded parking area in Fažana and have unlimited ferry travel to and from the island. There's a restaurant serving fish and meat dishes, plus a café for coffee and cakes.

Rovinj and around p25, map p26

€€€ Hotel Adriatic, P Budicin bb, T052-803510, www.maistra.hr. In the old town, overlooking the harbor, this is Rovinj's longest running hotel, dating from 1912. Renovated in 2005, the best of its 27 rooms have fine sea views. Breakfast is served on a waterside terrace out front.

€€€ Villa Valdibora, Chiurca Silvana 8, Rovinj, T052-845040, www.valdibora.com. In Rovinj's old town, this charming 17th-century villa has 5 2-room apartments, 3 studios and 3 double rooms, all with tile floors and wooden beamed ceilings. The apartments and studios also have well-equipped kitchenettes. There's a small gym, open to all guests.

€€ Casa Garzotto, Via Garzotto 8, T052-811844, www.casa-garzotto.com. In Rovinj's old town, this small boutique hotel offers four studios, 6 rooms and 2 suites in 4 separate 16th-century buildings. Expect wooden floors, antique furniture and kitchenettes several units also have open fires. Extras include free bike hire, plus sauna and hydro-massage shower in winter.

€€ Dva Baladura, Pilkovići 26/27, Kanfanar, T052-803 720, dvabaladura.hr. In Kanfanar, 12 km east of Rovinj, this peaceful family-run hotel is made up of traditional stone buildings and has 4 cosy rooms and 6 apartments, all with slick modern bathrooms. There's a restaurant serving delicious Istrian cuisine, a mini-wellness (sauna and massage), and a garden with an outdoor pool, making it an ideal choice for families with kids – though you will need a car.

€€ Stancija 1904, Smoljanci 2-3, Svetvinčenat, T052-560022, www.stancija.com. In the rural village of Smoljanci, 24 km east of Rovinj, this peaceful agrotourism venture occupies a beautifully restored stone farmhouse sleeping up to 8, while the 2 adjoining apartments sleep 2 and 4. They serve excellent meals prepared from local seasonal produce. It's set in lovely gardens with a covered terrace area for barbecues

and a small playground for kids, making a peaceful country alternative to touristy Rovinj.

€€ Villa Marea, Vukovarska 8, T052-811397, www.villamarea.com. Just a 20-min walk from the old town, this modern house has 2 double rooms, 8 studios and 3 apartments. The studios and apartments each come complete with a kitchenette. There's free Wi-Fi, bikes for hire and a pool.

€ La Grisa, Grisa 3, Bale, T052-824501, www.la-grisa.com. In the medieval hilltown of Bale, 12 km from Rovinj, this welcoming hotel opened in 2011. The 12 rooms and suites have wooden floors, exposed stonework and beams, and some have views across open countryside towards the sea. The excellent ground floor restaurant serves local meat and seafood specialities.

Poreč p27, map p28

€€€ Valamar Riviera Hotel & Residence, Obala M Tita 15, T052-465100, www.valamar.com. Fully renovated in 2010, this early 20th-century hotel (formerly known as Hotel Neptune) offers 105 smart rooms and suites. There's a sunny café-restaurant with tables out front overlooking the harbour in the old town – from here, regular taxi-boats run to the hotel beach on the nearby islet of Sveti Nikola. Some guests complain about the noise, but if it's central location you're looking for, this is definitely it.

€€ Hotel Hostin, Rade Končara 4, T052-408800, www.hostin.hr. Set among pine woods close to the bus station, just a 10-min walk from the marina and the old town, this smart, modern hotel is both central and peaceful. There are 39 spacious rooms, a buffet restaurant, and a wellness centre with an indoor pool, sauna, Jacuzzi and a gym.

€ Kaštel Pansion & Restaurant, Kaštelir, 7 km northeast of Poreč, T052-455310, www.kastel-kastelir.hr. This small, boutique hotel occupies a lovely 18th-century building with exposed stonewalls and wooden ceilings. There are 2 double rooms and 2 split-level suites, plus an excellent restaurant serving local specialities by an open fireplace.

€ **Villa Višnjan**, Kovačeva 9, T098-255063, www.villavisnjan.com. In the sleepy hilltown of Višnjan, 12 km from Poreč, this small hotel occupies a restored old stone building. There are 3 studios and 3 apartments (all with kitchens), plus 1 double room. Affording views over vineyards and olive groves, it is set in gardens with an outdoor pool and barbecue.

Motovun *p29*

€ **Hotel Kastel**, Trg Andrea Antico 7, T052-681047, www.hotel-kastel-motovun.hr. Occupying an 18th-century building just outside the town walls, this peaceful old-fashioned hotel has 29 rooms and three apartments. There's also a restaurant with open-air dining on a leafy terrace throughout summer, a wellness centre with an indoor pool, sauna and massage, plus an art gallery with temporary exhibitions by local and international artists.

€ **House of Gold**, Ulica Gradiziol 46, T052-681816, www.motovunaccommodation.com. In the old town, close to the main square, this medieval stone building has been carefully renovated and furnished in modern minimalist style. It has three guest rooms, plus a shared kitchen and living room.

€ **Villa Borgo**, Borgo, T052-681708, www.villaborgo.com. In Motovun's historic centre, close to the medieval town gate, this friendly B&B offers 10 basic but comfortable rooms and one apartment. Breakfast is served on a terrace with amazing views down onto the Mirna Valley.

Grožnjan *p30*

€€ **Hotel San Rocco**, Srednja ulica 2, Brtonigla, 15 km northwest of Grožnjan, T052-725000, www.san-rocco.hr. In the small village of Brtonigla, this small, family-run hotel was voted the Best Boutique Hotel in Croatia every year from 2007 to 2011. It occupies a beautifully restored old stone farmhouse and has 14 individually furnished guest rooms, most with wooden beamed ceilings. The highly regarded hotel restaurant serves local seasonal specialities in a dining room with exposed stonewalls and wooden floors. There's also a garden with an outdoor pool, and a small wellness centre with an indoor pool and sauna.

€ **La Parenzana**, Volpia 3, Buje, 14 km northwest of Grožnjan and 3 km from Buje, T052-725100, www.parenzana.com.hr. This beautifully restored old stone farmhouse has 16 comfortable guest rooms furnished with antiques and a large dining room with an open fire and summer terrace. Everything on the menu, including the wine, is organically produced on local farms. It is close to the disused Parenzana railway line, now a popular cycling route, and they have bikes for hire. They also arrange occasional Istrian cookery courses and wine-tasting tours.

€ **Villa San Vito**, Spinotti Morteani 2, T052-776113, www.villa-olea.com. On the edge of the old town, this 17th-century Baroque building was renovated in 2007. It has 2 cosy apartments with self-catering facilities, each sleeping 2, with extra beds available for kids. Guests are welcome to sit out in the orchard and use the barbecue area.

❼ Restaurants

Pula *p22, map p23*

€€ **Buffet Vodnjanka**, Dinka Vitezića 4, T052-210655. Just a 10-min walk from Pula's covered market, this family-run eatery serves up good old-fashioned home cooking. It's a great choice for lunch with the locals, with just a dozen or so tables, and daily specials such as mushroom ravioli, fried squid, and roast veal. Be sure to try the house wine, a crisp white Malvazija. Closed Sun.

€€ **Kantina**, Campo Marzio, Flanatička 16, T052-214054. Mon-Sat lunch and dinner, closed Sun. Near the covered market, Kantina has a dining room in a cosy cellar, plus outdoor tables on a terrace through summer. You get a free selection of dips and nibbles while you look through the menu, which features goodies such as ravioli filled with *pršut* (prosciutto) and goats cheese, and steak with truffles.

€€ Restaurant Scaletta, Flavijevska 26, T052-541599. Daily lunch and dinner. Taking up the ground floor of Hotel Scaletta (see Where to stay, page 31), near the Arena, this highly regarded restaurant serves sophisticated dishes such as gnocchi with salmon and gorgonzola, and steak stuffed with white truffles in a creamy sauce. There's a pleasant summer terrace just across the road.

€ Jupiter, Castropola 38, T052-214333, www.pizzeriajupiter.com. On the road leading up to the castle, this popular pizzeria has tables on a sunny open-air terrace through summer. There's a vast choice, but a good bet is a pizza diavolo (topped with spicy salami and hot chilli peppers) and a cold draught beer. Closed Mon.

Cafés and bars
Cvajner, Forum 2, T052-853465. This trendy but unpretentious café has open-air seating on Pula's Forum square through summer. Inside are frescoes uncovered during restoration, modern furniture and contemporary art, plus free Wi-Fi.

Rovinj and around *p25, map p26*
€€ Gostionica Toni, Driovier 3, Rovinj, T052-815303. Thu-Tue for lunch and dinner, closed Wed. For good, down-to-earth, Istrian home cooking, the house specialities at this informal, centrally located eatery are *brodet od sipe s palentom* (cuttlefish stew with polenta) and *njoki s dagnjama i rokulom* (gnocchi with mussels and rocket). Besides the standard menu, they also have daily specials on a board. It's in a narrow sidestreet, set back from the seafront.

€€ La Puntalina, Sv. Križa 38, T052-813186, In the old town, this smart family-run restaurant serves excellent local fresh fresh fish and seafood dishes on a stone terrace affording fine sea views. Downstairs, the cocktail bar (see Bars and clubs) comes under the same management, and is well worth a look in, either before or after your meal.

€€ Monte, Montalbano 75, T052-830203, www.monte.hr. Open Easter-Oct daily for lunch and dinner. In a terracotta-coloured house set in a lovely walled garden near the Church of St Euphemia, many now regard Monte as Rovinj's top restaurant. The ever-changing menu features creative cuisine prepared from locally sourced meat and seafood. To try a bit of everything, opt for the 5-course *degustacija* menu, which features 2 fish dishes, 2 meat dishes and a dessert. There's space for just 45 diners so reservations are essential.

€€ Restaurant Gianino, A Ferri 38, T052-813402. Open Apr-Oct Tue-Sun; Nov-Mar Fri-Sun. In a narrow side street, just back from the harbour, Gianino has long been popular with the yachting fraternity. House specialities include *tagliatelli mare-monti* (pasta with shrimps and mushrooms), rigatoni with lobster and sole with truffles.

€€ Veli Jože, Sv Križa 1, T052-816337. Open Apr-Nov for lunch and dinner. This highly popular, informal eatery serves old-fashioned local dishes such as *bakalar in bianco* (a pâté made from dried cod) and roast lamb with potatoes.

€€ Viking, Svet Lovreč, Limski Kanal, T052-448119. Closed Jan. Ranked among Istria's top restaurants, this large establishment is best known for its fresh oysters, pasta with shrimps and mushrooms and barbecued fish dishes.

€ Da Sergio, Grisia 11, T052-816949. In a narrow cobbled side street leading up to the hilltop Church of St Euphemia, Sergio's is generally regarded as Rovinj's best pizzeria. Come here for reasonably priced, delicious, thin-crust pizzas, comparable to the best in Italy. Try the 'Istrian', topped with tomato, and local prosciutto, sheep's cheese and olives.

Cafés and bars
Viecia Batana, Trg M Tita 8. Rovinj's oldest and most atmospheric café stands on the main square, close to the harbour. Perfect for coffee.

Poreč *p27, map p28*

€€€ Ulixes, Decumanus 2, T052-451132. Daily lunch and dinner. In the old town, just off the main thoroughfare, this cosy *konoba* has a centuries-old stone-and-brick interior and a pretty courtyard garden. Come here for pasta dishes, fresh fish, salads and local wines – but remember that you'll be paying for the central location as well as for the food.

€€ Dvi Murve, Grožnjanska 17, T052-434115, www.dvimurve.hr. Daily lunch and dinner. A short distance northwest of Poreč, this *konoba* is consistently ranked among the best in Istria. Expect tasty dishes such as beefsteak Dvi Murve (steak with cream, mushroom and ham sauce), and *brancin u soli* (sea bass baked in a salt crust).

€ Pizzeria Nono, Zagrebačka 4, T052-434173. Daily lunch and dinner. Opposite Poreč's tourist office, Nono remains busy with locals throughout the year. It's much loved for its delicious pizzas baked in a brick oven, plus pasta and gnocchi dishes, steaks and colourful salads.

Motovun *p29*

€€ Mondo Konoba, Barbican 1, T052-681791. This cosy *konoba* (formerly known as Barbican) serves traditional Istrian dishes with an innovative twist. It has an airy dining room with wooden tables, and serves up goodies such as pasta with truffles, steaks and colourful seasonal salads.

€€ Pod Voltom, Trg Josefa Ressela 6, T052-681923. Thu-Tue lunch and dinner. Closed Wed. On the main square in Motovun's old town, close to the tourist office, this homely eatery has an exposed brick interior with an open fire. It's known for *fuži* (Istrian pasta) with truffles, steak with truffles, and local game dishes. In the summer they have outdoor tables with the best view in town, and terrific sunsets.

Grožnjan *p30*

€€ Bastia, 1 Svibnja, T052-776370. This eatery serves up hearty dishes in a cosy dining room with an open fire in the old town. Try the tagliatelle carbonara, made with huge chunks of crisp pancetta, or a generous platter of mixed grilled meats.

€€-€ Agroturizam Dešković, Kostanjica 58, 5 km from Grožnjan, T052-776315, www.vina-deskovic.hr. This traditional stone cottage has a dining room with an open fireplace and red-and-white checked tablecloths. The house specialities are home-made pasta and roast veal – all the ingredients are locally sourced and the olive oil, wine and *rakija* are made by the Dešković family themselves.

€ Kaya Energy Bar, Vincenta iz Kastva 2, T091-4433430. In the old town, this beautifully designed café serves breakfast, as well as excellent wine by the glass and platters of local cheese. Take a table outside on the stone terrace, for amazing views over the surrounding countryside.

Hum *p30*

€€ Humska Konoba, Hum 2, T052-660005. May-Oct daily lunch and dinner, Mar-Apr Tue-Sun, Nov-Feb Sat-Sun. This tiny, old-fashioned *konoba* with an open fireplace has been serving typical home-made Istrian dishes since 1976. Expect *fuži* (a type of pasta) with truffles or goulash, home-made sausages, and *biska*, a local liquor made from mistletoe.

🎵 Bars and clubs

Pula *p22, map p23*

Rock Club Uljanik, Dobrilina 2, www.club uljanik.hr. Thu-Sat 2100-0600. A thriving venue for alternative rock concerts, in a disused building overlooking the shipyard, close to the city centre. On the go since 1965.

Uliks, Trg Portarata 1, T052-219158. A popular little bar looking onto the Triumphal Arch of the Sergi. It's next door to the house where James Joyce once lived, hence the life-size sculpture of the writer himself sitting outside.

Rovinj and around p25, map p26

La Puntalina, Sv. Križa 38, T052-813186.
In the old town, below the restaurant of
the same name, this romantic cocktail bar
serves drinks at cushions nestled into the
rocks, overlooking the sea. Great sunsets too.
Valentino, Sv Križa 28, T052-830 683,
www.valentino-rovinj.com. Daily 1800-0100.
Extremely popular cocktail and champagne
bar by the water's edge in the old town, with
cushions so you can sit on the rocks. Very
romantic at sunset.

Poreč p27, map p28

Byblos, Zelena Laguna, T091- 6633312,
www.byblos.hr. May-Sep, Wed-Sat 2300-0500.
The largest nightclub in the region, playing
predominantly house music with guest DJs
from New York and London – David Guetta
and Erick Morillo have played here.
Epoca, Obala M Tita 24, T052, www.epoca.hr.
Open all day till late, for coffee, drinks
and cocktails, you'll find this café on
the seafront promenade, close to the
Valamar Riviera Hotel.

✹ Festivals

Pula p22, map p23

Late Jul Pula Film Festival, www.pulafilm
festival.hr. Founded in 1954, this 2-week
competitive festival is held in the Arena and
at Kaštel, and features films from both Croatia
and abroad. It attracts international names
from the world of cinema – Jeremy Irons and
Christopher Lee have attended in the past.
Late Jul Seasplash Festival, www.sea
splash.net. 4-day reggae festival by the
sea at Fort Punta Christo, Štinjan, near
Pula, with free camping included in the
price of the ticket.
Late Aug Outlook Festival, www.outlook
festival.com. 4-day dubstep festival, by the
sea at Fort Punta Christo, Štinjan, near Pula.
Early Sep Dimensions Festival,
www.dimensionsfestival.com. 4-day
underground electronic festival, by the sea
at Fort Punta Christo, Štinjan, near Pula.

Poreč p27, map p28

Jul Aug Classical Music Festival,
www.concertsinbazilika.com. Sacral and
secular music in the Basilica of St Euphrasius.
Jul Aug Jazz in Lapidarium, www.jazzinlap.
com. Jazz festival held in the courtyard
of the town museum, attracting classical
and contemporary performers from the
international scene.

Motovun p29

Late Jul Motovun Film Festival,
www.motovunfilmfestival.com. 5-day
international festival of avant-garde cinema,
founded in 1999. They also organize an eco-
camp with showers and toilets and regular
shuttle buses to Motovun old town.

Grožnjan p30

Mid-Jul Jazz is Back, www.jazzisbackbp.com.
This 3-week open-air jazz festival attracts big
names, both from Croatia and abroad.

◎ Shopping

Pula p22, map p23

Aromatica, Laginjina 4, T052-382180,
www.aromatica.hr. Close to the Arch of the
Sergi, this store stocks its own line in natural
soaps and cosmetic products made from
olive oil and scented with wild herbs.
Tržnica, Narodni Trg. Mon-Sat 0700-1330,
Sun 0700-1200. Pula's market combines a
steel-and-glass pavilion selling meat and
fish, plus a stall selling fruit and vegetables
on the square.

Rovinj and around p25, map p26

Aromatica, Garibaldi 20, T052-812850,
www.aromatica.hr. In the old town, this
store offers the same products as its sister
shop in Pula, above.
Sheriff & Cherry, Carera 6, www.sheriffand
cherry.com. This store stocks its own brand
of handmade vintage-inspired sunglasses
with quality lenses. Tasteful and original,
they're also available at Harvey Nichols,
Liberty and Joseph in London.

Motovun *p29*

Zigante Tartufi, Gradiziol 8, Motovun, T052-681668, www.zigantetartufi.com. Part of the Zigante chain, this is the place to purchase truffles and truffle products from the Mirna Valley, plus Istrian olive oil and wines.

Grožnjan *p30*

Zigante Tartufi, U Gorjan 5, Grožnjan, T052-776099, www.zigantetartufi.com. This shop offers the same services as the branch in Motovun, above. It also offers wine and truffle tasting.

⏱ What to do

Pula *p22, map p23*
Diving
Diving Indie, Camping Indije, Banjole 96, T052-573658, Banjole (10 km south of Pula), www.istradiving.com.

Food and wine
Activa Travel, Scalierova 1, T052-215497, www.activa-istra.com. 1-day and 3-day wine-tasting tours, departing from Pula.

Rovinj and around *p25, map p26*
Boat trips
Delfin Excursions, Zagrebačka 5, T091-5142169, www.excursion-delfin.com. Runs daily boat trips from Rovinj to Poreč, calling at the Lim Fjord en route, with a seafood lunch included.

Cycling
Vetura, Šetalište vijeća Europe, T052-815209, www.vetura-rentacar.hr. Rents bikes. A marked bike path runs along the coast south of town from the ACI Marina, passing through Zlatni Rt, Rt Kuvi, Veštar and Cisterna to arrive in Sv Damijan. A map, Bike Track Rovinj, is available from the tourist office. See also istria-bike.com.

Diving
Rovinj Diving, Marija Trošt 6, Delnice, T051-816203, www.rovinj-diving.hr.

Poreč *p27, map p28*
Boat trips
Marco Polo, Poreč harbour, T091-2017474, www.marco-polo-excursion.com. Runs daily boat trips from Poreč to Rovinj, departing at 1000, calling at the Lim Fjord en route, with a lunch included.
Vetura, Zelena Laguna, T052-451391, www.vetura-rentacar.hr. Rents bikes. Note that Poreč is the starting point for 2 well-marked bike routes: one north to Tar (45-km round trip) and the other south to Funtana (47 km). Ask at the tourist office for details and a map or check the website, istria-bike.com.

Diving
Diving Centar Poreč, Brulo 4, T052-434606, www.divingcenter-porec.com.

Inland Istria *p29*
Cycling
Montona Tours, Kanal 10, T052-681970, Motovun, www.montonatours.com. Rents bikes and help visitors plan cycling tours of Inland Istria, including accommodation en route.

Food and wine
Zigante Tartufi, Livade 7, Livade, T052-664302, www.zigantetartufi.com. Arranges 3-hr truffle-hunting trips complete with dogs in the Mirna Valley region. Tours are possible Oct-Dec for white truffles and Jan-Sep for black truffles. Lunch is included.

⊖ Transport

See also Transport in Istria and Kvarner, page 8.

Pula *p22, map p23*
Bus
From Pula, frequent buses run to **Rijeka** (2 hrs 20 mins); **Zagreb** (4 hrs); **Zadar** (7 hrs); **Split** (10 hrs) and **Dubrovnik** (14 hrs).

Train
From Pula there are 3 trains daily to **Rijeka** (2½ hrs) with a change at Lupoglav.

Rovinj and around *p25, map p26*
Bus
From Rovinj, regular buses to **Pula** (45 mins) and **Poreč** (45 mins).

Poreč *p27, map p28*
Bus
From Poreč there are regular buses to **Pula** (1¼ hrs) and **Rovinj** (45 mins).

❶ Directory

Pula *p22, map p23*
Hospital   Zagrebačka 30, T052-376000, www.obpula.hr. **Pharmacy**   Each pharmacy (www.istarske-ljekarne.hr) is marked by a glowing green cross. The pharmacy at Giardini 15, T052-222551, works 24 hrs.

Rovinj and around *p25, map p26*
Hospital   There is a special tourist surgery at the Ambulanta Rovinj at Istarska ulica bb, T052-813004. **Pharmacy**   Each pharmacy is marked by a glowing green cross. **Gradska Ljekarna**, M Benussi, T052-813589, open summer 0800-2100.

Poreč *p27, map p28*
Hospital   Dom Zdravlja (Medical Centre), M Gioseffija 2, T052-451611, 0700-2100. **Pharmacy**   Each pharmacy is marked by a glowing green cross. **Centralna Ljekarna**, Dom Zdravlja, M Gioseffija 2, T052-434950, is the most central. If closed, there will be a notice on the door saying which pharmacy to go to.

Contents

Footprint features

Kvarner

Rijeka

Overlooking the Kvarner Gulf, Rijeka is Croatia's largest port, with a shipyard, massive dry dock facilities, refineries and other heavy industries. Architecturally, the centre is remarkably similar to Trieste in Italy, with a grid of grandiose 18th-century Austro-Hungarian buildings on the seafront, and a sprawling suburb of high-rise apartment blocks from the 1960s. The main public meeting place is the Korzo, a pedestrian street a couple of blocks back from the port, lined with shops and open-air cafés. There are few memorable sights here, other than the lovely hilltop castle and pilgrimage church of Trsat, and the city has only a limited number of hotels – most visitors prefer to stay in the nearby

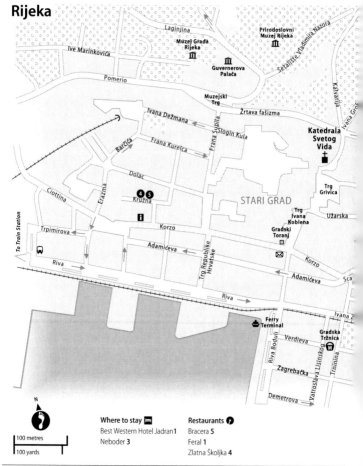

Rijeka

Laginjina
Ive Marinkovića
Pomerio
Prirodoslovni
Muzej Rijeka 🏛
Muzej Grada
Rijeka 🏛
🏛 Guvernerova
Palača
Šetalište Vladimira Nazora
Kalvarija
Ivana Dežmana
Muzejski
Trg
Žrtava fašizma
Ivana Grom
Frana Supila
Barčića
Frana Kurelca
Slogin Kula
Katedrala
Svetog
Vida ✝
Dolac
Erazma
Ciottina
Kružna 🟦🟦
ℹ️
STARI GRAD
Trg
Grivica
Trg
Ivana
Koblena
Užarska
To Train Station
Trpimirova
Korzo
Gradski
Toranj
Adamićeva
Trg Republike
Hrvatske
✉️
Korzo
Riva
Adamićeva
Sca
Riva
Ivana Z
🚢 Ferry
Terminal
Verdieva
Gradska
Tržnica 🏪
Riva Boduli
Zagrebačka
Vatroslava Lisinskog
Timinina
Demetrova

N

100 metres
100 yards

Where to stay 🛏
Best Western Hotel Jadran **1**
Neboder **3**

Restaurants 🍴
Bracera **5**
Feral **1**
Zlatna Školjka **4**

seaside resorts of Opatija and Lovran. Rijeka receives national television coverage each year for the staging of Croatia's largest carnival.

Arriving in Rijeka

Getting there The bus station is a five-minute walk west of the city centre at Žabica 1, T060-302010, autotrans.hr. **Jadrolinija**, www.jadrolinija.hr, runs daily ferries from Rijeka to Cres Town (Cres) and Mali Lošinj (on Lošinj), plus a daily catamaran from Rijeka to Rab Town (Rab), which then continues to Novalja (Pag, North Dalmatia). A coastal ferry also runs several times weekly from Rijeka to Dubrovnik, stopping at Split and the Dalmatian islands of Hvar and Korčula en route. The train station a 10-minute walk west of the city centre at Krešimirova 5, T060/333-4444, www.hznet.hr.

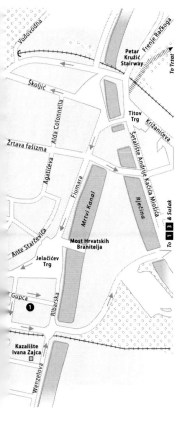

Tourist information Rijeka's walk-in Tourist Information Centre (TIC) is at Korzo 14, T051-335882, www.tz-rijeka.hr.

Korzo

A couple of blocks inland from Rijeka's Riva (seafront), this main pedestrian thoroughfare was created in the 18th century, when the city extended beyond the medieval city walls. Today, lined with clothes shops and open-air cafés, it is Rijeka's main shopping street and public meeting space. The name Korzo comes directly from the Italian, *Corso*.

Pomorski i Povijesni Muzej

ⓘ *Muzejski trg 1, T051-213578, www.ppmhp. hr, Jun-Sep Tue-Fri 0900-2000, Sat 0900-1300, Oct-May Tue and Thu-Fri 0900-1600, Wed 0900-2000, Sat 0900-1300, 10Kn.*

A 10-minute walk northeast of the centre, on the hillside facing down towards the port, the neo-Renaissance Governor's Palace houses the Maritime and History Museum. Downstairs you'll see archaeological finds, period furniture and clocks and paintings, while the second floor is devoted to local shipping, with a display of model ships, navigational instruments, anchors, charts and old photos.

Most hrvatskih branitelja

ⓘ *Fiumara bb.*

The elegant Memorial Bridge to Croatian Soldiers crosses the Mrtvi Kanal (Dead Canal) east of the town centre. Built in 2002,

Zvončari

Unique to the carnival in Rijeka and the surrounding villages, Zvončari are young men dressed in bizarre costumes consisting of a sheepskin slung over the shoulders, a mask of a grotesque animal head with horns, and a large iron bell tied around the waist. During the afternoons and evenings, in the week preceding Shrove Tuesday, they go from village to village and house to house in large groups, regardless of the weather, acting roguishly and making a dreadful din with their bells. Traditionally, locals offer them *fritule* (similar to small doughnuts) and wine, then see them on their way. Their purpose is to chase away the forces of evil and invite the coming of spring and new life.

its minimalist design features clean lines in metal and glass; at night, thanks to subtle lighting effects, it appears to float on the water. While most Croatian towns commissioned heroic sculptures to honour local soldiers who fell during the war of independence, Rijeka chose to build this pedestrian bridge instead, symbolizing the city's high regard for tolerance. It was designed by Studio 3LHD from Zagreb and has won various international architectural awards.

Pilgrimage path to Trsat
ⓘ *Titov trg.*
Up on the hill, 139 m above the town, stand the Church of Our Lady of Trsat and Trsat Castle. You can walk up following the pilgrimage path – a steep but worthwhile climb of over 500 steps brings you up through the dramatic Rječina Gorge. A baroque gateway marks the beginning of the stairway, which starts from Titov Trg on the left bank of the River Rječina. At the top, turn left and follow the busy road of Šetalište Joakima Rakovca uphill to arrive at Frankopanski Trg. If you don't feel up to the hike, take bus No 2 or 8 from the city centre.

Gospa Trsat
ⓘ *Frankopanski Trg, T051-452900, daily 0700-1900.*
The Church of our Lady of Trsat was built to commemorate the 'Miracle of Trsat', when angels were said to have carried the house of the Virgin Mary from Nazareth and delivered it on this spot in 1291. As the story goes, it remained here for three years and was then moved (by the angels again) to Loreto, near Ancona in Italy.

Inside the church, above the altar, an icon of the Virgin Mary, sent as a present from Pope Urban V in 1367 to console the people of Trsat for the loss of the holy house, is hung with offerings from pilgrims such as pearl necklaces and trinkets.

Next to the church, inside the Franciscan Monastery, the Chapel of Votive Gifts displays an extraordinary collection of offerings brought here by pilgrims, including a painted wooden sculpture of the Virgin and Child, countless religious portraits and even discarded crutches, proof of the Virgin's miraculous healing powers.

Trsatska Gradina (Trsat Castle)
ⓘ *Ulica Zrinskog, T051-217714, Jun-Sep daily 0900-2000, Oct-May daily 0900-1700, 10Kn.*
A five-minute walk from Frankopanski Trg, Trsat Castle was built in the Middle Ages on the foundations of a Roman observation point. In 1826 the remains of the castle were bought by Laval Nugent, an eccentric Irishman who had served in the Austrian army. He had it

restored in romantic style, and added a Classical Greek temple with four Doric columns brought from Pula, intended as the family mausoleum. There's a gallery with a permanent exhibition tracing Trsat's history, and in summer an open-air café, offering amazing views over the city and across the Kvarner Bay to the islands of Cres and Krk.

Around Rijeka

Opatija

Opatija, 15 km west of Rijeka, is Croatia's longest-standing tourist resort with its old-fashioned hotels and an ageing clientele – through winter and spring at least half the guests are over 60. The seafront hotels, built largely in Viennese Secessionist style, offer neat gardens and sunny terraces where you can drink coffee and watch the world go by during the day; through summer dinner is also served outside, often accompanied by live music. The tourist office is at Vladimira Nazora 3, T051-271710, www.opatija-tourism.hr.

In the early 20th century, Opatija was one of Europe's most elegant and fashionable seaside destinations. Illustrious visitors included royalty and artists: Emperor Franz Josef, Wilhelm II of Germany and Prussia, the Italian opera composer Giacomo Puccini, the Irish novelist James Joyce and the American dancer Isadora Duncan all came here.

Lovran-Opatija-Volosko
ⓘ *Šetalište Franza Josefa.*
This 12-km coastal footpath, lined with century-old oaks and cypress trees, runs from Volosko to Lovran, passing through the seaside towns of Opatija, Ičići and Ika en route. Construction began in 1885, coinciding with the opening of Opatija's first hotels. It makes a lovely walk, with plenty of places to stop for a drink or a snack on the way.

Lovran
Pretty Lovran, 21 km west of Rijeka, gives onto the Kvarner Gulf and is backed by the surging rocky mass of Mount Učka (1396 m). Many people prefer it to Opatija, and indeed it is more authentic, with a medieval centre, a harbour and a number of fish restaurants. On the edge of town, set amid lush gardens overlooking the seafront promenade, stands a row of elegant late 19th-century villas, several of which have been converted into luxury holiday apartments.

Risnjak National Park
ⓘ *Information centre, Bijela Vodica 48, Crni Lug, T051-836133, www.risnjak.hr, 40Kn.*
Fifteen kilometres inland from the coast, the forested heights of Risnjak National Park make a pleasant contrast to Kvarner's seascapes. In summer the air is refreshingly cool and through winter the craggy peaks are snow-covered. Two-thirds of the park is covered with dense beech and fir while the rest supports mountain meadows.

The best place to start exploring the park is the picturesque little village of Crni Lug (726 m), 40 km northeast of Rijeka. Here, just a few minutes west of the park administration building, you'll find the beginning of the Leska Educational Trail, a 4.2-km circular route with information points in both Croatian and English. Also from Crni Lug, a well- marked hiking path leads to the highest peak, Veliki Risnjak (1528 m). Allow three hours each way, wear substantial walking boots and take plenty of water.

The Risnjak forests form a natural habitat for the lynx, after which the park is named (lynx in Croatian is ris). Other wild animals here include the brown bear, wildcat, roe deer, red deer and chamois, plus the seldom-sighted wolf and wild boar. Risnjak is home to over 50 bird species, too including the capercaillie, the largest type of European grouse.

Island of Krk

Linked to the mainland by a 1430-m bridge, and home to Rijeka Airport, Krk is one of the most accessible of all the Croatian islands. It also happens to be the largest (38 km long and 20 km wide) and one of the most populous.

While the northwest part of the island is low lying, fertile and fairly developed, the southeast part is mountainous and in places quite barren. It's certainly not the most beautiful island on the Adriatic, but its accessibility and wealth of tourist facilities make it very popular.

The chief centre is Krk Town, which dates back to Roman times, with a 12th-century seafront castle and a cathedral. Punat, home to the largest marina on the Adriatic, is a haven for yachters, while Vrbnik is known for its excellent white wine, Vrbnička Žlahtina. The best beach, Vela Plaža is in Baška.

Arriving on Krk

Getting there There are regular buses from Rijeka bus station (Žabica 1, T060-302010, www.autotrans.hr) to Krk Town, Punat and Baška. **Jadrolinija**, www.jadrolinija.hr, operates daily ferries from Valbiska (Krk) to Merag (Cres). **Linijska Nacionalna Plovidba**, www.lnp.hr, operates daily ferries from Valbiska (Krk) to Lopar (Rab).

Tourist information There is a general Krk Island tourist office in Krk Town at Trg sv Kvirina 1, T051-221359, www.krk.hr. Krk Town has a tourist information office at Vela Placa 1/1, T051-221414, www.tz-krk.hr.

Katedrala Uznesenja

ⓘ *Trg Sv Kvirina, Krk Town, daily 1000-1300, 1700-1900.*
Taking on its present form during the 12th century, the Cathedral of Our Lady of the Assumption was built on the site of an early Christian basilica, which grew up over the first-century Roman baths. Ancient stone columns, topped with finely carved capitals, were incorporated into the structure, and a Gothic chapel dedicated to the wealthy Frankopan family was added in the 15th century.

Adjoining the cathedral, the 12th-century Romanesque Church of St Quirinus (same hours as the cathedral) is split into two levels, with a lower crypt area where prisoners sentenced to death attended a final Mass before execution. The church's treasury displays works of religious art including a stunning silver-plated altarpiece depicting Virgin Mary in Glory (1477) made in Venice as a gift for the cathedral.

Punat and the Islet of Košljun

On Krk's southwest coast, Punat is a launching pad for visiting the nearby Islet of Košljun with its 15th-century **Franciscan Monastery** ⓘ *T051-854017, Mon-Sat 0930-1700, Sun 1030-1230, 20Kn boat transfer, plus 20Kn admission.* Inside, a museum display includes paintings, model ships, and a collection of local folk costumes, with a set of ladies' scarves, each one indicating which village the wearer came from and her marital status. Košljun was home to one of the first European financial institutions: the Košljun Lending House, which was set up to protect the poor from usurers, and functioned between the 17th and 19th centuries. Puňat tourist office is at Pod Topol 2, T051-854860, www.tzpunat.hr.

Baška

Baška, 19 km southeast of Krk Town, is the oldest and best-known resort on the island. Its main attraction is **Vela Plaža**, a 1.8-km stretch of pebble and sand, one of Croatia's most spectacular beaches. However, it does get very busy, with the tourist office estimating space for 5000 bathers. If you prefer something more peaceful, take a taxi boat to any one of the succession of small, secluded bays (accessible only from the sea) west of town. Baška itself has few cultural attractions, and what was once a compact fishing village now straggles almost 3 km along the coast, due to the hotels, apartments and eateries that have sprung up over the last 35 years. Baška tourist office is at Kralja Zvonimira 114, T051-856817, www.tz-baska.hr.

Vrbnik

Vrbnik, 10 km east of Krk Town, is a tiny, tightly packed medieval walled settlement, standing on the edge of a limestone cliff, 48 m above the sea. Most visitors come here specifically for the wine cellars, which stock the highly esteemed, dry, white Vrbnička Žlahtina. The best place to taste it is **Nada** (see Restaurants, page 54).

Island of Cres

Sparsely populated and little explored by the average tourist, this long, skinny, mountainous island is joined to a second island, Lošinj, by a bridge. The northern end is covered by a dense deciduous forest of beech and oak, known as the Tramunatana, which gradually gives way to meagre pastures and barren landscapes in the south. More for those in search of unspoilt nature rather than culture, Cres offers good opportunities for hiking and birdwatching (the rare Eurasian griffon vulture nests here), but little in the way of art and architecture. The islanders live primarily from sheep farming: *Creška janjetina* (Cres lamb) is especially tasty thanks to the clean pastures, rich in wild herbs such as *kadulja* (sage).

Arriving on Cres

Getting there For buses to and from Cres Town, contact Rijeka bus station, T060-302010, www.autotrans.hr. For regional bus travel, see page 8. **Jadrolinija**, www.jadrolinija.hr, operates daily ferries from Rijeka to Cres Town, Brestovo (Istria, mainland) to Porozina (Cres), and from Merag (Cres) to Valbiska (Krk). In summer only, a catamaran operates between Rijeka and Mali Lošinj, stopping at Cres Town en route.

Tourist information Cres Town has a tourist information office at Conc 10, T051-571535, www.tzg-cres.hr.

Cres Town

The island's chief settlement is made up of pastel-coloured houses giving on to a broad seafront promenade, which cuts its way around a deep triangular harbour filled with small fishing boats. Fortified in the 16th century, the old town is made up of a maze of winding streets opening out onto small squares. The seafront promenade leads west of town to a stretch of coast offering a series of small coves ideal for sunbathing and swimming.

The Tramuntane and Eco-center Caput Insulae

ⓘ *Beli 4, Beli, 20 km north of Cres Town, T051-840525, www.supovi.hr, Mar-Oct daily 0900-2000, 40Kn, the eco-centre can arrange special birdwatching tours on request.*

Eurasian griffon vultures

The Eurasian griffon vulture is one of the world's largest flying birds, with a wingspan of up to 2.8 m, a body weight of up to 15 kg, a maximum speed of 120 kph and eyesight nine times better than a human. It feeds on animal carcasses but never attacks living animals, and has long been respected by the farmers of Cres as it prevents disease by eating the bodies of dead sheep. However, as the island has seen a gradual but continual trend of depopulation, so the number of farmers and sheep has declined, and the griffon has been left with little in the way of food.

During the 1980s, when the number of griffon vultures had dropped to less than 50, the Eco-centre Caput Insulae established several feeding sites, where they deposit carcasses of slaughtered sheep and rescue injured birds so they can be taken to the centre and treated.

Their numbers have since risen, and there are now about 70 couples nesting in colonies on the vertical cliffs on the northeast side of the island. The female lays one egg per year, and during the two-month period of incubation both parents sit on the egg. After hatching, the chick grows in the nest for four months, then spends another couple of months learning to fly with it parents, after which it leaves for several years roving, travelling as far as a field as Greece, Israel and Spain. At the age of five, the griffon returns to the cliff where it was born, finds a mate and builds a nest, and then lives in the vicinity of its birthplace for up to 60 years.

However, modern-day life remains a constant threat to these spectacular birds. They occasionally chance upon carcasses of vermin that have been intentionally poisoned, they have a tendency to fly into electric cables, and young birds may even lose control of their wings and fall into the sea if disturbed by tourists during the summer season.

The Nature Conservation Act has declared the Eurasian griffon vulture a protected species. The killing or disturbing of griffon vultures, and the stealing of their eggs or chicks, are offences liable to a penalty of up to 40,000Kn. The public display of stuffed griffon vultures is also illegal.

In an isolated and semi-abandoned cluster of old stone cottages on the edge of the Tramuntane forests, you'll finds the Eco-center Caput Insulae. There's an informative exhibition, Biodiversity of the Archipelago of Cres and Lošinj, and a reserve for injured Eurasian griffon vultures. From here, seven eco-trails lead through the surrounding forests – it's well worth picking up an illustrated booklet at the information centre, to help you identify the trees and plants as you go. In fact Cres is one of the richest ornithological areas on the Adriatic – you can expect to see birds such as golden eagles, snake eagles, honey buzzards and, of course, griffon vultures.

Island of Lošinj

Smaller but much more densely populated and certainly more touristy than neighbouring Cres, Lošinj is known for its mild climate, lush vegetation and the long-established resort of Mali Lošinj.

Arriving on Lošinj

Getting there For buses to and from Mali Lošinj, contact Rijeka bus station, T060-302010, www.autotrans.hr. **Jadrolinija**, jadrolinija.hr, operates daily ferries from Rijeka to Mali Lošinj and from Mali Lošinj to Zadar (North Dalmatia). In summer only, a catamaran operates between Rijeka and Mali Lošinj, stopping at Cres Town en route. In addition, Emilia Romagna Lines, emiliaromagnalines.it, run catamarans between Lošinj and Cesenatico, Pesaro and Rimini (Italy), late June to early September.

Tourist information Mali Lošinj has a tourist information office at Riva Lošinjskih Kapetana 29, T051-231884, www.tz-malilosinj.hr.

Mali Lošinj

At the end of a sheltered, elongated bay on the southwest coast, Mali Lošinj is the largest settlement on all the Croatian islands. Despite its name, it's far bigger than neighbouring Veli Lošinj (*mali* means small, *veli* large). Everyday life focuses on the harbour, skirted by a seafront promenade lined with cream, ochre and russet façades, many housing street-level cafés with open-air seating under colourful awnings through summer. The town's loveliest houses, set in lush gardens filled with Mediterranean planting, were built by retired sea captains during the 19th century. Through peak season the place is packed with visitors, most of whom sleep in the large, modern hotels on Čikat Peninsula, joined to the centre by a coastal path that meanders its way between the turquoise blue sea and scented pinewoods.

Veli Lošinj

Veli Lošinj is a little fishing town of pastel-coloured houses built around a bay. It's quieter and more authentic than its neighbour, but still has a few things worth seeing, a selection of fish restaurants and a **Marine Education Centre** ① *www.blue-world.org, Jul-Aug daily 1000-2100; May, Jun and Sep Mon-Fri 1000-1600, Sat 1000-1400; Oct-Apr Mon-Fri 1000-1400, 15Kn*, dedicated to researching a local school of bottle-nosed dolphins.

Island of Rab

Rab is probably the most beautiful of all the Kvarner islands. While the windswept northeast side is rocky and barren with steep cliffs plummeting down to the sea, the sheltered southwest part is gently undulating and covered with dense, green pinewoods. The main reason for coming here is to explore medieval Rab Town, an architectural treasure perched on a walled peninsula, rising high above the sea. There are also some blissful stretches of sandy beach on the northern coast at Lopar, so you can combine sightseeing with swimming and sunbathing, not to mention the excellent fish restaurants. Rab is a particularly popular destination for Germans and Hungarians, being one of the easiest islands to access from Central Europe.

Arriving on Rab

Getting there Jadrolinija, jadrolinija.hr, operates a daily catamaran from Rijeka to Rab Town, which then continues to Novalja (Pag, North Dalmatia). **Linijska Nacionalna Plovidba**, www.lnp.hr, operates daily ferries from Lopar (Rab) to Valbiska (Krk).

Tourist information Trg Municipium Arbe 8, T051-724064, www.tzg-rab.hr.

Rab town

The old town can be divided into two parts: the medieval stone cottages of **Kaldanac** – on the tip of the peninsula – and **Varoš**, which takes up the land end of the peninsula and is made of paved streets lined with 15th- to 17th-century Gothic and Renaissance buildings. The old town has three streets (Donja Ulica, Srednja Ulica and Gornja Ulica), which run parallel to the waterfront promenade. The main cultural monuments are on **Gornja Ulica**, the upper street, and you'll find standard tourist haunts on **Srednja Ulica**, the middle street, where street artists set up their easels in peak season.

Trg Municipium Arbe Rab's main square opens out onto the seafront, half-way along the peninsula. It's rimmed with cafés and the tourist office is also here. The main monument is the **Kneževi Dvor** (Rector's Palace), built between the 13th and 16th centuries.

Crkva Sv Marije Velike ⓘ *Ivana Rabljanina, T051-724195, Jun-Sep 1000-1300 and 2030-2200, Oct-May open only for Mass or on request, Treasury 5Kn.* Standing on the highest point of the peninsula is the 12th-century Romanesque Church of St Mary the Great. The façade is made up of pink and white stone, and decorated with rows of Romanesque blind arches to each side of the main portal.

Rab Town

Where to stay ▣
Arbiana **4**
Grand Hotel Imperial **1**
Pansion Tamaris **5**

Restaurants ⓪
Astoria **2**
Konoba Rab **1**
Santa Maria **3**

Veli Zvonik ① *Ivana Rabljanina, Jun-Sep 1000-1300, 1930-2130, Oct-May closed, 10Kn.* A short distance from the Church of St Mary the Great, the free-standing, 13th-century Great Bell Tower is the tallest (25 m) and most beautiful of Rab's four campanili. You can climb to the top for views over the town and the surrounding seascapes.

Crkva Sv Justina ① *Gornja Ulica, closed for restoration.* St Justine's Church houses a Museum of Sacred Art. Top exhibits are an ornate 13th-century silver-plated box containing the skull of St Christopher (the town's patron saint), and a mid-14th-century polyptych by Paolo Veneziano. The church bell tower, topped with an onion dome, dates from 1672.

Bazilika Sv Ivana Evandeliste ① *Gornja Ulica, daily, free.* Probably originating from the early Christian era, the Basilica of St John the Evangelist, now in ruins, was abandoned in the early 19th century. Today, all that remains is the 12th-century bell tower, which was restored in 1933 and stands 20 m high.

Rab Town's beaches The most central places to swim and sunbathe are on the west side of Komrčar Park. Through summer, taxi boats shuttle visitors to and from Frkanj Peninsula, west of Rab Town, where there are plenty of rocky coves backed by woods, as well as the nudist beach of Kandarola.

Lopar Peninsula
On the northern tip of the island, the sparsely populated Lopar Peninsula boasts some of Croatia's sandiest beaches. Here you'll find the island's largest and most popular family beach, **Rajska Plaža** (Paradise Beach), a 1.5-km stretch of sand backed by restaurants and cafés. A 15-minute walk north of Rajska Plaža is the nudist beach of **Stolac**, while an even more remote nudist beach, **Sahara**, is found in the peninsula's northernmost bay.

Kvarner listings

For hotel and restaurant price codes and other relevant information, see pages 10-15.

⊖ Where to stay

Rijeka *p40, map p40*

€€ Best Western Hotel Jadran, Šetalište XIII divizije 46, T051-216600, www.jadran-hoteli.hr. On the coast, 15-min walk from the city centre, the Jadran has 69 rooms affording fantastic sea views. They do a generous buffet breakfast, and there's a small beach area out front with sunbeds and parasols.

€ Neboder, Strossmayerova 1, T051-373538, www.jadran-hoteli.hr. This 1930s modernist high-rise building (the name means 'skyscraper') has 14 floors. Renovated in 2007, it has 54 small but comfortable rooms, most with a balcony and stunning views over the city and the sea, plus a café serving drinks and snacks. You'll find it in the Sušak area, just across the river from the centre of Rijeka, about 1 km from the port.

Around Riejka *p43*

€€ Hotel Balatura, Mali Sušik 2, Tribalj, Crikvenica, 30 km southeast of Rijeka, just off the coastal road down to Dalmatia, T051-455340, www.hotel-balatura.hr. Stay at this lovely ethno-hotel to escape the masses. It occupies a restored 300-year-old stone manor house. It has 8 rooms and 2 suites, all decorated in subtle colours with exposed stonewalls, traditional furniture and details such as big paintings used to hide the flat-screen TVs. There's also a courtyard restaurant.

Opatija and around *p43*

€€ Villa Ariston, Maršala Tita 179, T051-271379, www.villa-ariston.com. This late 19th-century villa, set in a lovely garden running down to the seafront promenade, attained its present appearance during the 1920s. It has 8 luxury guest rooms and 2 suites, each with parquet flooring and antique furniture. There's an excellent restaurant on the ground floor, and many non-residents come here to eat.

€ Ika Hotel, Primorska 16, Ika, T051-291777, www.hotel-ika.hr. Between Opatija and Lovran, on the seaside promenade, this small, family-run hotel has 17 rooms and a seafood restaurant with a terrace looking over the water, plus a small beach. Open Apr-Oct.

€ Stancija Kovačici, Rukavac 51, Matulji, T051-272106, www.stancija-kovacici.hr. Hidden away in the hills, a 10-min drive from Opatijia, this peaceful B&B offers 5 rooms, all well furnished and with decent a/c, plus an excellent restaurant serving local dishes and wine.

Lovran and around *p43*

€€€ Hotel Villa Astra, Viktora Cara Emina 11, T051-294400, www.lovranske-vile.com. This Secessionist villa is set in lush gardens overlooking the sea. It has 6 beautifully furnished suites, a restaurant serving organic cuisine, a spa with a flotation tank and an outdoor heated pool with a bar. The owners, Lovranske Vile, also have several other properties in the area.

€€ Hotel Draga di Lovrana, Lovranska Draga 1, T052-294166, www.dragadilovrana. hr. High up on the slopes of Mt Učka, 7.5 km from Lovran, affording spectacular views down onto Kvarner Bay, this building dates from 1910. Since 2005, it has operated as a small hotel with just 4 rooms and one luxurious top-floor apartment (with an open fire, jacuzzi and sauna). On the ground floor there's a very popular smart restaurant serving gourmet cuisine, plus a smaller, more informal *konoba* (rustic-style restaurant) serving local specialities.

€€ Hotel Lovran, Šetalište Maršala Tita 19/2, T051-291222, www.hotel-lovran.hr. Composed of 2 early 20th-century villas, joined together by a modern reception area, this hotel is set in a lush park overlooking the sea. It has 50 rooms (most but not all with air conditioning) and 3 suites, a restaurant, a small wellness centre with sauna and gym, plus two tennis courts.

Risnjak National Park *p43*
€ Hotel Risnjak, Lujzinska 36, Delnice, T051-508160, www.hotel-risnjak.hr. On the go since the 1930s, this hotel reopened in 2004 after a complete renovation. There are 21 rooms and one suite, a cosy rustic restaurant and café, plus a fitness centre. They offer a wide range of adventure sports including hiking, rafting and paragliding, and have mountain bikes to rent.

Island of Krk *p44*
€€ Hotel Bor, Šetalište Dražica 5, Krk Town, T051-220200, www.hotelbor.hr. A 5-min walk along the seafront from the old town, this hotel dates back to 1920 and was renovated in 2002. There are 18 simple but comfortable rooms and 4 suites, plus a front terrace with a bar-restaurant and outdoor seating below the pine trees, giving onto a rocky bathing area.
€€ Marina Hotel, Ružmarinska 6, Krk Town, T052-221357, www.hotelikrk.hr. Right on the seafront in the centre of Krk, Marina Hotel is close to the cathedral and dates back to 1925. Renovated in 2008, it is now an upmarket 4-star hotel with just 7 rooms and 3 suites, each with modern minimalist furniture, fabrics in shades of yellow and brown, plus a balcony and sea view. The ground-floor restaurant has a lovely waterside terrace.

Punat and the islet of Košljun *p44*
€€ Kanajt, Kanajt 5, T051-654340, ww.kanajt.hr. This small hotel occupies the former 16th-century Bishop's Palace overlooking Punat marina. Renovated in 2004, it has 20 simple but comfortable rooms and 2 suites, all with carpets and standard 1980s furniture, plus a restaurant with a front terrace serving excellent local seafood and lamb. Popular with sailing types, it also offers a charter service.

Baška *p45*
€€ Hotel Tamaris, Emila Geistlicha bb, T051-864200, www.baska-tamaris.com. Overlooking Baška's fine pebble beach, this hotel has 15 spacious rooms and 15 apartments, all simply but smartly furnished. The hotel restaurant serves Mediterranean cuisine on a large sea-view terrace. It's noted for its friendly and helpful staff.

Vrbnik *p45*
€€ Apartments Nada, Ulica Glavača 22, T051-857065, www.nada-vrbnik.hr. These 2 beautifully restored old stone houses are owned by the people who run Nada (see Restaurants, page 54). Apartment Božanić is located within Vrbnik's medieval town walls, and has a kitchen and living room (sofa bed) with a fireplace, a double bed on a mezzanine level, plus a barbecue and jacuzzi in the garden. Apartment Zameniljak lies just outside town, set amid dense Mediterranean planting, and has an open-plan kitchen with a beamed ceiling and fireplace, 3 double rooms, 2 bathrooms, and an outdoor jacuzzi.
€ Hotel Argentum, Supec 68, T051-857370, www.hotel-argentum.net. This 10-room modern hotel is a short walk from the old town. It has a good restaurant with a terrace looking out to sea, and it makes an ideal base for a couple of days.

Island of Cres *p45*
€€ Hotel Kimen, Melin I/16, Cres Town, T051-573305, www.hotel-kimen.com. Refurbished in spring 2008, a 2-km walk along the coast from the centre, is Cres Town's only hotel. All the 128 basic but comfortable rooms have a balcony, Wi-Fi and a bathroom. A wellness centre offering sauna, solarium and gym opened in summer 2009. Popular with tour groups, it arranges excursions such as a Gastro Tour, Eco Tour, Hiking and Olive Picking.

€ MaMaLu, Valun 13a, Valun, T051-525035, www.mamalu-valun.hr. Besides good food, this welcoming family-run seafood eatery offers several basic but comfortable rooms, all with sea views. You get a generous breakfast on the waterside terrace, a decent beach nearby, and the option of eating dinner here too, with everything prepared using locally produced olive oil and wine.

€ Pansion Tramontana, Beli, T051-840519, www.beli-tramontana.com. Close to the eco-centre and an ideal base for exploring the Tramuntane forests, this friendly family-run B&B has 7 double rooms, 3 triple rooms and 2 family rooms, and a restaurant serving local lamb and seafood. The same family run a scuba diving centre based on a nearby beach.

Island of Lošinj *p47*

€€ Hotel Kredo, Gortana 9, Čikat, T051-233595, www.kre-do.hr. Overlooking the sea and backed by pinewoods in Čikat, a 15-min walk from Mali Lošinj town centre, this villa offers 9 rooms and 2 apartments. Expect wooden floors, simple but tasteful furnishing, plus a smart kitchenette in the self-catering units. There's a waterside bar-restaurant, a mini wellness centre, plus bikes for hire and boat transfers to nearby beaches.

€€ Hotel Manora, Nerezine, T051-237460, www.manora-losinj.hr. Away from the busy tourist areas, family-run Manora is in Nerezine, 25 km north of Mali Lošinj. Located just a 10-min walk from the harbourfront, it has 22 double rooms, plus a restaurant, sauna, massage, a gym, and a garden with a small pool.

€€ Hotel & Restaurant Televrin, Obala nerezinskih pomoraca, Nerezine; T051-237121, www.televrin.com. In the yellow former town hall building dating from 1910, on Nerezine harbourfront, this 3-star hotel has 13 double rooms and 2 suites. Downstairs, local seafood and lamb dishes are served in a loggia with an open fireplace overlooking the sea.

€€ Villa Favorita, Sunčana uvala bb, Mali Lošinj, T051-520640, www.villafavorita.hr. With a view of the sea and backed by pinewoods, this Secessionist building has been restored to form a small hotel with 8 double rooms. There's also a bar, sauna and outdoor pool filled with sea water set in a garden.

€ Villa Mozart, Kaciol 3, Veli Lošinj, T051-236262, no website. In a 19th-century sea captain's house overlooking the harbour, this welcoming B&B offers basic but comfortable rooms (with a/c), plus an informal ground floor restaurant.

Island of Rab *p47, map p48*

€€ Arbiana, Obala Petra Krešimira IV, Rab Town, T051-775900, www.arbianahotel.com. Standing on the harbour front, this building dates back to 1924. Now a lovely boutique hotel offering the best accommodation in town, it has 28 rooms with sumptuous furnishing and sweeping curtains. Known for its friendly staff and personal service, it also has a highly regarded restaurant and stays open all year.

€€ Grand Hotel Imperial, Palit bb, Rab Town, T051-724522, ww.imperial.hr. Rab Town's oldest hotel sits on the edge of the old town, amid the greenery of Komrčar Park. The 134 rooms are smart and modern and a decent buffet breakfast is served in the hotel restaurant. The town beach lies just a 10-min walk away and the hotel operates taxi boats (free) to Frkanj nudist beach.

€€ Pansion Tamaris, Palit 285, T051-724925, www.tamaris-rab.com. Overlooking the sea in St Euphemius Bay in Palit, this friendly little hotel has just 14 rooms plus a restaurant serving excellent seafood on a pleasant terrace. You can walk through Komrčar Park to be in Rab Town in just a few minutes, and there are taxi boats from the jetty to the beaches on Frkanj Peninsula.

🍴 Restaurants

Rijeka *p40, map p40*

€€ Feral, Matija Gupca 5b, T051-212274, www.konoba-feral.com. Mon-Sat lunch and dinner, Sun lunch only. Friendly, unpretentious and reasonably priced, this seafood eatery occupies and 18th-century building with an exposed stone and brick interior, and ceilings hung with fishing nets. Try the *riblja juha* (fish soup) followed by fish (choose which fish you want from a platter and they will cook it for you). It's popular with locals and stages occasional live music in the evenings.

€€ Kukuriku, Trg Lokvina 3, Kastav, T051-691519, www.kukuriku.hr. On a small square in the medieval village of Kastav, 11 km west of Rijeka, this gourmet restaurant serves creative Mediterranean cuisine prepared from local seasonal ingredients – expect dishes such as cream of pumpkin soup, and veal medallions with brie. It also doubles as a stylish boutique hotel with 15 rooms and suites.

€€ Zlatna Školjka, Kružna 12a, in a side street off the Korzo, T051-213782, www.zlatna-skoljka.hr. Mon-Sat lunch and dinner, closed Sun. Serves creative seafood dishes in a pastel-coloured dining room with a combination of modern furniture and antiques. Cosy and reliable.

€ Bracera, Kružna 12, T051-213782, www.pizzeria-bracera.com.hr. Daily lunch and dinner. Rijeka's favourite pizzeria is opposite the more upmarket fish restaurant, Zlatna Školjka.

Opatija and around *p43*

€€ Le Mandrać, Obala F Supila 10, Volosko, 4 km from Opatija, T051-701357, www.lemandrac.com. Daily lunch and dinner. Opened in 2004 and now regarded as one of Croatia's best restaurants, Le Madrać is housed in a minimalist glass conservatory with ambient music, candles and a sea view. There's a special 'slow food' menu consisting of 9 courses including delicacies such as foie gras, truffles and oysters.

€€ Plavi Podrum, Obala F Supila 12, Volosko, 4 km from Opatija, T051-701223, www.plavipodrum.com. Daily lunch and dinner. This classic seafood restaurant has a formal dining room and outdoor tables overlooking a pretty fishing harbour. It's noted for excellent fresh fish and an outstanding wine list.

Lovran and around *p43*

€€ Dopolavoro, Učka 6, Ičići, T051-299641, www.dopolavoro.hr. Daily lunch and dinner. On the old road up Mt Učka, at an altitude of 1000 m, Dopolavoro's front terrace affords great views down onto Kvarner Bay. Come here for hearty local meat dishes such as venison, wild boar and lamb, as well as seasonal specialities including wild mushrooms, asparagus and truffles.

€€ Najade, Šetalište Maršala Tita 69, T051-291866. Daily lunch and dinner. This restaurant has long been popular with Croatians, who come here to eat fish on a terrace overlooking the sea. It's close to the harbour, and the owner reputedly gets first choice of the catch when the fishermen come in.

Island of Krk *p44*

€€ Konoba Šime, Antuna Mahnića 1, Krk Town, T051-220042. Daily lunch and dinner. 1 block in from the Riva, on the left as you pass through Mala Vrata, this typical *konoba* is noted for tasty, reasonably priced pasta dishes.

€€-€ Bracera, Kvarnerska 1, Malinska, T051-858700, www.konoba-bracera.com. Daily lunch and dinner. In Malinska, 13 km north of Krk Town, this friendly eatery is run by an owner-chef who also catches the seafood on offer. Food is prepared over an open fire in the old-fashioned dining room, which has a wooden-beamed ceiling hung with fishing nets and old fishing tools, plus heavy wooden tables and benches.

Punat and the Islet of Košljun *p44*

€€€ Marina, Puntica 9, T051-654380. Daily lunch and dinner. Based in the marina with a view over the bay and the Islet of Košljun, this highly regarded restaurant serves up local specialities.

Baška *p45*

€€ Cicibela, Emila Geistlicha 22a, T051-856013, www.cicibela.hr. Daily lunch and dinner. This cosy restaurant is known for its discreet waiters and romantic atmosphere. There's a good selection of fish and seafood dishes, with pizza providing a cheaper option.

Vrbnik *p45*

€€ Nada, Ulica Glavača 22, T051-857065, www.nada-vrbnik.hr. Daily lunch and dinner. Close to the harbour, Nada doubles as a restaurant, where you can eat fresh fish and seafood on a terrace with views out to sea, and a *konoba*, where you can sample the *Žlahtina Nada* along with nibbles such as *ovči sir* (sheep's cheese) and *pršut* (smoked ham). Reservations recommended. By prior agreement you can also visit their main wine cellars (Zagrada 4, below the town walls) for a guided tour, a video presentation and wine tasting.

Island of Cres *p45*

€€ Belona, Šetalište 20 Aprila 24, Cres Town, T051-571203. Daily lunch and dinner. This old-fashioned eatery is known for oven-baked *arbun* (sea bream), pasta with lobster, and oven-baked lamb with potatoes. In warm weather eat outside on the terrace.
€€ Konoba Bukaleta, Loznati, T051-571606. Daily lunch and dinner. In the mountains, 5 km from Cres Town, this modern white building has a large terrace affording fine views over the Kvarner Gulf. Widely regarded as the best eatery on the island, the speciality here is local Cres lamb, prepared in a variety of ways: roast lamb, lamb goulash with gnocchi, lamb's liver and so on. They also serve sheep's cheese and

home-baked bread. Be sure to reserve a table in advance during high season.

Island of Lošinj *p47*
Mali Lošinj

€€ Artatore, Artatore 132, Uvala Artatore, T051-232932, www.restaurant-artatore.hr. Daily lunch and dinner. Located 7 km north of Mali Lošinj, this restaurant is especially popular with yachters, who moor up in front of the terrace overlooking the bay. The owner does the cooking himself and his top dishes are *škampi rižot* (shrimp risotto), *jastog s rezancima* (lobster with pasta) and *ribe na žaru* (barbecued fish).
€€ Pizzeria Draga, Braće Vidulića 77, T051-231132. Daily lunch and dinner. This friendly, bustling restaurant offers a range of pasta dishes and salads at lunchtime, and in the evenings adds a vast choice of brick-oven baked pizzas to the menu. There's a covered terrace area so you can eat outside.

Veli Lošinj

€€ Bora Bora, Rovenska 3, T051-867544, www.borabar.com. Daily lunch and dinner. In Rovenska Bay near Veli Lošinj, funky Bora Bar is run by an Italian-born owner-chef who is married to a Croatian. Expect modern Mediterranean cuisine using local produce, with an emphasis on seafood and truffles, plus fresh home-made pasta. Popular with sailing types, there are water and electricity connections for boats out front, as well as Wi-Fi.
€€ Mol, Rovenska 1, Veli Lošinj, T051-236008. This family-run seafood restaurant has tables by the water's edge, overlooking the bay where local fishing boats moor up in the evening. Try the *dagnje na buzaru* (mussels cooked in garlic, wine and parsley) followed by either *brodet* (fish stew served with polenta) or barbecued fresh fish, along with a bottle of excellent Malvazija white wine.

Island of Rab *p47, map p48*

€€ Astoria, Dinka Dokule 2, Rab Town, T051-774844, www.astoria-rab.com. Daily lunch and dinner. On the 1st floor of Residence Astoria, this up-market restaurant has a terrace overlooking Rab's main square and the harbour. The menu features local meat and fish dishes using organic ingredients and fresh herbs.

€€ Konoba Rab, Kneza Branimira 3, Rab Town, T051-725666. Daily lunch and dinner. In a side street running between Srednja Ulica and Gornja Ulica, this *konoba* serves up meat and fish prepared either on a barbeque or under a peka.

€€ Nada, Palit 201, T051-724845, www.rab-restaurant-nada.com. Popular with locals and visitors alike, this family-run seafood restaurant lies on the coast, a 10-minute walk from Rab Town. It dates from 1973, with tables arranged on a pretty terrace, and favourite dishes including *crni rižot* (black risotto made from cuttlefish ink) and the mixed fish platter for 2 (including 1 sea bass, 1 gilthead bream, and a handful of shrimps and squid). The owners have their own fishing boat, so everything is freshly caught.

€€ Santa Maria, Dinka Dokule 6, Rab Town, T051-724196. In the old town, in the atmospheric courtyard of an old stone building, this restaurant serves classic Croatian fare. Start with *dagnj na buzaru* (mussels cooked in garlic, white wine and parsley), followed by a tuna steak, and round off with a slice of *Rabska torta* (Rab cake, made from almonds and lemon).

🎵 Bars and clubs

Rijeka *p40, map p40*
Boa, Ante Starčevića 8, Rijeka, T091-339 9339, www.clubboa.com. Slick lounge-bar playing mainstream music, with occasional guest DJs and special events.
Indigo, Stara Vrata 3, T051-325300, www.indigo.com.hr. In the old town, this lounge-restaurant-bar has a pop feel.

Nina 2, Adamićev Gat, T091-531 7879, www.nina2.com. In a boat on Rijeka's seafront, DJs playing house and R&B.
Palach, Kružna 6, T051-215063. In a street off the Korzo, grungy Palach has been hosting the city's top rock concerts for over 25 years.
Stereo Dvorana, Strossmayerova 1, Rijeka. Nightclub and concert venue, staging performances by both local and foreign bands.

Opatija *p43*
Disco Seven, Maršala Tita 125, Opatija, T051-711781. On the seafront in Opatija, this summer disco plays house music.

🎊 Festivals

Rijeka *p40, map p40*
Hartera Festival, www.hartera.com. 3-day festival of alternative music, featuring international bands, staged in a former paper factory in late Jul.
Rijeka Karneval, see page 16.

Opatija *p43*
Liburnia Jazz Festival, www.liburniajazz.hr. 3-day annual jazz festival, attracting international names, held in early Jul.

Lovran *p43*
Each year, Lovran organizes 3 gastro-food festivals, during which the town's restaurants prepare dishes based on seasonal delicacies. The **Dani Šparoga** (Asparagus Festival) takes place in **Apr**; **Dani Trešanja** (Cherry Festival) in **Jun** and **Marunada** (Chestnut Festival) **late Sep-early Oct**.

🛍 Shopping

Rijeka *p40, map p40*
Aromatica, Medulićeva 5a, T051-321061, www.aromatica.hr. In a side street, a couple of blocks back from the Korzo, this store stocks its own line in natural soaps and creams, made from olive oil and scented with wild herbs.

Covered Market, Demetrova 3. Mon-Sat 0700-1400, Sun 0700-1200. Dating from the late 19th century, the halls of the covered market offer Rijeka's most enjoyable shopping experience – be sure to check out the fish market, complete with art nouveau details.

Rab Town *p48, map p48*
Vilma, Trg Sv. Kristofora bb, T051 724 537, www.rabskatorta.com. This bakery specializes in Rabska torta (Rab cake, made from almonds and lemon), a local speciality that dates from 1177, and was reputedly invented to honour the Pope's visit to the island.

☼ What to do

Rijeka *p40, map p40*
Ad Natura, Ivana Filipovića 6, Rijeka, T091-590 7065, www.adnatura.hr. Organizes mountain biking, free climbing and kayaking in the mountains of Risnjak and Učka.

Island of Krk *p44*
Squatina Diving Centre, Zarok 88a, Baška, T051-856034, www.squatinadiving.com.

Island of Cres *p45*
Diving Club Beli, Pansion Tramontana (see Where to stay), T051-840519, www.diving-beli.com.

Island of Lošinj *p47*
Diving Center Sumartin, Sv. Martin 41, T051-232835, www.sumartin.com.

Island of Rab *p47, map p48*
Aqua Sport, Supetarska Draga 331, T051-776145, www.aquasport.hr.
Moby Dick, Lopar 493, T051-775577, www.mobydick-diving.com.

⊖ Transport

See also Transport in Istria and Kvarner, page 8.

Rijeka *p40, map p40*
Bus
Frequent buses run to **Zagreb** (2½ hrs), **Pula** (2 hrs 20 mins), **Zadar** (4 hrs), **Split** (7 hrs) and **Dubrovnik** (11 hrs).

Train
From Rijeka several trains run daily to **Zagreb** (4 hrs).

❶ Directory

Rijeka *p40, map p40*
Hospital   Krešimirova 42, near Rijeka train station, T051-658111, www.kbc-rijeka.hr.
Pharmacy   Each pharmacy is marked by a glowing green cross. Ljekarna Centar, Riva 18 (T051-213101) and Ljekarna Korzo, Korzo 22 (T051-211036) work alternate 24-hr shifts.

Contents

Background

History

The Illyrians and Greek and Roman colonization

The earliest known inhabitants of the region are the Illyrians, who settled along the Adriatic coast and its hinterland during the Bronze Age. They were divided into various tribes – Liburnians, Histri and Delmati – and built simple hilltop settlements fortified with stone walls.

The Greeks started colonizing the coast in the fourth century BC. The first settlement, Issa, was founded by inhabitants of the Greek colony of Syracuse (Sicily) on the island of Vis, and included a theatre with a capacity for 3000 spectators. Issa later became independent, and founded several more colonies such as Tragurion (Trogir) and Lumbarda (on the island of Korčula). Local Illyrians traded jewellery, metalwork, glassware, salt, wine and oil with the Greeks, and thus Greek colonization induced the development of craftsmanship, the building of towns and more sophisticated farming.

In the mid-third century BC, the southern tribes united to form an Illyrian state, living in part from piracy. Feeling threatened by Illyrian expansion, the Greeks called the Romans for help. When Roman messengers arrived to ask the Illyrians leader, Queen Teuta, to curtail piracy, they were promptly put to death, causing the beginning of a series of wars between the Romans and the Illyrians. In 167 BC, the Illyrian state was defeated and its territory turned into the Roman province of Illyricum.

The first Roman settlers were traders and soldiers. Legions built military camps, roads, bridges and aqueducts, which stimulated the arrival of civilians attracted by the possibility of expanding trade and colonization. This lead to the development of the coastal towns of Pola (Pula), Jader (Zadar), Salona (Solin) and Epidaurum (Cavtat). Croatia's best-preserved Roman monuments are the Arena (amphitheatre) in Pula, and Diocletian's Palace in Split.

When the Roman Empire was divided into the Eastern and Western Empires in AD 395 – a division that was to have far-reaching consequences for the later history of the Balkans – Dalmatia fell within the West. With the fall of the Western Empire in AD 476, the region became part of the Ostrogoth state, then in AD 555 it was made a Byzantine province. During the second half of the sixth century, it was invaded by tribes of Slavs and Avars, who travelled south through Dalmatia, where they demolished Salona.

According to the Byzantine Emperor and historian Constantine Porphyrogenitus, the Croats were invited to present-day Croatia by Emperor Heraclius (AD 575-641) to expel the Avars. This they did, also defeating other Slavic tribes, and they soon became the dominant force in the former Roman province of Dalmatia.

The development of a Croatian state

Very few written documents exist regarding the Croats' early years in the region, although around the year AD 800 we have evidence of one Duke Višeslav, whose court was based in Nin, near Zadar, in North Dalmatia.

Croatian territory covered the hinterland of the coastal towns of Zadar, Trogir and Split, but did not include these towns. It stretched south as far as the River Cetina (near Omiš), and east into Bosnia, and later extended north to include Istria. When the Croatian rulers were at their height, Pannonia was also part of Croatia.

Trpimir, Duke of Croatia (AD 845-864), is deemed as the founder of the dynasty that ruled the country until the end of the 11th century. He considered the entire territory his own property and surrounded himself with a council of hand-picked *župani* (counts), each responsible for a *županije* (county), to help him rule. Trpimir's successor, Domagoj (AD 864-876), built up Croatia's naval strength and came into conflict with Venice over control of the Adriatic. After Domagoj, Zdeslav (AD 878-879) came to power but he was assassinated and was succeeded by Branimir (AD 879-882) who was loyal to the Pope and obtained the first international recognition of Croatia from Pope John VIII.

At that time the 'Apostles of the Slavs', the brothers Methodius and Cyril, were requested by the Byzantine emperor to invent an alphabet for the Slavic languages, thereby spreading the Byzantine influence among these people. The papacy, worried about the strengthening of Byzantium, wanted to keep Croatia under Rome's watch.

The following century is linked with Tomislav's reign (AD 910-928). He started his rule as a *dux* (duke) but changed his title to that of *rex* (king) around AD 925. For his victories over the Bulgarians, the Byzantine emperor awarded him control over the Dalmatian towns and the title of 'proconsul' so he could rule them in the name of the Byzantine Empire. Tomislav defeated the Hungarians and united Coastal and Pannonian Croatia.

In 1054 the 'Great Schism' (the break between Eastern and Western Christian churches) took place, and the border between the Eastern and Western Roman Empires, drawn up in AD 395, became the border between the Roman Catholic and Orthodox churches. The east Adriatic, bisected by this border, was of direct interest to both the Pope in Rome and the patriarch in Constantinople. The papacy was eager to keep Croatia under the Catholic wing.During the rule of Petar Krešimir IV (1058-1074), two church councils met in Split, proclaiming sanctions against clergy who gave sermons in the Croatian language, had beards, were married or in any other way resembled the Eastern Church. Krešimir was recognized as the King of Dalmatia and Croatia by the Pope, and thus the Byzantine theme of Dalmatia was truly united with Croatia. Krešimir was not just a Byzantine official like Tomislav and Tomislav's successors, he was the absolute leader of the entire region.

However, soon after Krešimir's death a conflict blew up, provoked by the Normans, Venetians, Byzantines, Hungarians and the Pope in Rome, who all hoped to gain control over Croatia and Dalmatia. The result was that Zvonimir, the former ban (governor) at the time of Krešimir, succeeded to the throne in 1075 and took the title King of Croatia and Dalmatia. Zvonimir was chosen thanks to the support of Pope Gregory VII, and in return he placed the country under papal sovereignty.

After Zvonimir, Stjepan Trpimirović ruled for a short time, but he was too weak to put an end to difficult internal problems. This chaos was used by the Hungarians to take control of Croatia and Dalmatia and finally fulfil their long desire to open up their land-locked territories with access to the sea. Rome favoured the Hungarians, and so in 1091 Hungarian King Ladislas succeeded in taking Pannonia (which from then on became known as Slavonia) too. In 1102, Ladislas' successor, Koloman, oversaw the signing of the Pacta Conventa, in which the heads of the 12 most powerful Croatian families recognized him as their leader, and accompanied him to Biograd-na-Moru (near Zadar) where he was crowned King of Croatia and Dalmatia.

Austro-Hungary, the Turks and Venice

Croatian history from 1102 until 1991 finds the country divided into three administrative areas that had little contact with each other – Croatia, Slavonia and Dalmatia – under various foreign powers.

In the 14th century, the Ottoman Turks began expanding towards Croatia. The Holy Roman Emperor and King of Hungary, Sigismund I (1387-1437) organized a crusade against the Turks, but was defeated at the Battle of Nicopolis in 1396. It was an evil omen that signified the forthcoming wars between Croatia and the Ottoman Empire that would last for centuries.

After the fall of neighbouring Bosnia in 1463, the Croatian borderlands lay open to Turkish attack. The first defeat took place in Lika in 1493, when the Turks achieved victory over the Croatian army. Constant Turkish attacks on Croatian lands brought great disruption. Peoples from Serbia and Bosnia fled the Turks, seeking refuge in Croatia, and these migrations affected food production, resulting in poverty and famine. Croatia's western neighbours, namely Venice and the Hapsburgs, recognized the danger for their own countries and started worrying about how to defend Croatia in order to defend themselves. By the end of the 15th century, conflicts between the ruling Hungaro-Croatian aristocracy culminated in the aristocracy opposing the king and the lower nobility, and the burghers opposing the clergy. In 1526, a catastrophic defeat of the Hungarian army by the Turks at the Battle of Mohacs brought about the problem of electing a new king, as Louis II had somewhat ignominiously drowned in a river as he tried to escape the battle.

On 1 January 1527, the Croatian nobles elected Ferdinand Hapsburg as their king. He thus became the leader of Croatia, Dalmatia and Slavonia, and the entire territory was absorbed into the Holy Roman Empire of the German people. At the time the Hapsburgs were the kings of Czech, Hungary, Spain, the Netherlands, Naples and even Mexico.

To defend the region against the Turks, the Hapsburgs established the *Krajina* (military border) in the 16th century. In 1578, work began to build Karlovac as a major defence nucleus – Turkish skulls were thrown into the foundations of Karlovac as a sign of the mood of the times. Other defence posts were later built to the south and east. To guard these positions, a special borderline army was formed, made up largely of Vlahi, Orthodox Serb cattle farmers who had fled the Turks from the east. By this time the Hapsburgs were overriding the authority of the *ban* (Croatian governor) and the *sabor* (Croatian parliament), and the *Krajina* was put under German officers who took their orders directly from Vienna.

The rule of the first Hapsburgs was devoted to defending the region against the Turks. When the Turks took Klis in 1537, they effectively had control over the entire Dalmatian hinterland all the way south to the River Neretva, leaving Dalmatia divided between Venice and the Ottoman Empire. In October of the same year, the Turks defeated Ferdinand's armies in Slavonia, and thus opened their way to the Croatian lands in the west.

The Turks achieved their greatest victories at the time of Sultan Suleiman the Magnificent (ruled 1520-1566). On his campaign against Vienna, his army was detained by the Croatian *ban*, Count Nikola Zrinski, and his army at Szeged (southern Hungary). Even though Szeged was eventually conquered in 1566, Zrinski's heroic defenders aroused doubts about Turkish invincibility. In 1593, the Turks suffered defeat near Sisak, marking the beginning of a 13-year war against Croatia and Hungary. This war ended with a peace treaty in 1606, proving the decline of Turkish power. During the first half of the 17th century, the Croatian nobles considered that the *Krajina* (military border) had fulfilled its task, and demanded that it should come back under the authority of the Croatian *ban*.

The *Krajina* had physically divided Croatian territory in two, which made national integration difficult. The Emperor's Court in Vienna had two reasons not to disband the military border: on the one hand, it was an infinite source of cheap, well-trained, loyal soldiers and, on the other hand, Vienna feared that national integration would strengthen the Croatian aristocracy. The Hapsburgs decided to keep the border soldiers to serve their own interests.

During the 200-year fight to hold back the Turks, Croatia lost not only three-quarters of its territory, but also the same proportion of its population. People either died in battle, or were captured by the Turks and taken away to be used as slaves. The survivors moved to the north and the west of the country, and even beyond its borders. The aristocracy also migrated northwards, thus displacing the centre of the Croatian state from Coastal Croatia to Upper Croatia.

Two Croatian aristocratic families in particular distinguished themselves in the wars against the Turks: the Frankopans and Zrinskis. These two families were related by blood and held similar political beliefs. In the 17th century, Petar Zrniski, together with a group of Hungarian aristocrats, lead a mission to free Croatia of Hapsburg domination. But the conspiracy was discovered and Vienna sentenced Petar Zrinski and his brother-in-law Franjo Frankopan to the guillotine. They were executed on 30 April 1671, and their extensive estates became property of the Hapsburgs.

By 1718, Croatia had reclaimed all of Slavonia and much of Lika from the Turks. The Hapsburgs did not want to strengthen Croatia, so on the pretext of having been won in war, these lands were placed under military authority, effectively becoming part of the *Krajina*. The Hapsburgs also started to give away large estates in liberated Slavonia to foreign (German and Hungarian) families, to the obvious detriment of the Croatian nobility. Therefore, the Croatian parliament became disaffected, and fewer and fewer noblemen participated in its meetings, attending the Hungarian parliaments instead, where they solved Hungaro-Croatian matters together with the Hungarian nobles.

Ironically, with the expulsion of the Turks, Croatia's position became even more uncomfortable, as the Hapsburgs tightened their grip on the country. By this time a sizeable Serbian population (of the Orthodox faith) were living in Croatia, and when Russia began to show interest in the situation, the so-called Eastern Question evolved: when the Turks finally left the Balkans, who would rule, Catholic Austria or Orthodox Russia? Later this would be one of the factors that contributed to the escalation towards the First World War.

Another powerful empire also held Croatian lands: Venice. By the mid-16th century, the Turks had conquered all of Dalmatia apart from the islands and the coastal cities of Zadar, Šibenik, Trogir and Split, which were under Venetian control. By the late 17th century, Venice had extended its territory along the entire coast and into the hinterland. The Venetians applied the name Dalmatia to all these parts and, like the Hapsburgs, declined to return territories liberated from the Turks to the Croatian aristocracy.

In 1718, the peace treaty of Požarevac awarded Venice the hinterland territory eastwards up to the Dinara Mountains and south to Kotor (in present-day Montenegro). The Independent Republic of Dubrovnik now found itself surrounded by Venetian territory. However, the citizens of Dubrovnik were very skilful diplomats and, not wanting the Venetians as neighbours, they gave the area to the north around Klek (present-day Neum) and the area south around Sutorina (close to Herceg Novi in Montenegro) to the Turks, thus forming a buffer zone between the republic and the Venetian Empire.

This was later to cause great difficulties in defining the geographical limits of Croatia. The borders of today's Croatia were drawn up according to the peace treaty in Požarevac.

As Bosnia and Herzegovina remained under the Ottoman Turks until 1878, part of the territory of medieval Croatia is now western Bosnia, and the area around Neum has been awarded to Bosnia as access to the sea, thus cutting across the Croatian coast. Croatian nationalists have always resented this; during the war of the 1990s Tudjman described Croatia as a croissant-shaped country that needed a filling.

The arrival of Napoleon and the eventual fall of the Hapsburgs

With the demise of the Venetian Empire in 1797, Dalmatia was handed to the Hapsburgs. In 1806, Napoleon took Dalmatia, bringing to the region a series of progressive reforms, but also imposing hefty taxes and recruiting local men to participate in his army and navy. In 1809, Napoleon united Dalmatia with parts of Slovenia and Croatia, calling the new region the Provinces Illyriennes (Illyrian Provinces). During the Napoleonic Wars, the English navy defeated the French fleet near Vis, and subsequently took the island from 1811 to 1815, using it as an important strategic base on the Adriatic. After Napoleon's downfall in 1815, Dalmatia came back under the Hapsburgs.

In 1827, a new law was passed making the Hungarian language obligatory in all Croatian secondary schools. As a reaction against increasing Germanization and Hungarianization of the region under Austro-Hungary, Ljudevit Gaj (1806-1872) founded the Illyrian Movement. Gaj believed that unification of the South Slavs was essential, and aimed at doing this through a reawakening of the national consciousness, primarily through language and literature. Gaj's movement was renamed the National Party in 1843, the name Illyrian having been prohibited.

The National Party rapidly gained popularity on county assemblies and as a counter-Hungarian wing in the parliament. The ideas the Illyrians cherished were expressed in the so-called 'Demands of the People', which included the union of Dalmatia, Slavonia and the *Krajina* (military border), the institution of Croatian as the official language, and the foundation of a Croatian people's army.

The National Party also voted for Josip Jelačić as *ban* (governor), and he was instated on 4 June 1848. Croatia was now in a difficult position because the revolutionary movement in Hungary refused any possible agreement with the Croats. The Hungarian revolutionary leader, Lajos Kossuth, famously said: "Where is Croatia? I do not see it on the map." In September 1848, Jelačić thus lead his army into battle with the Hungarian revolutionaries, in the defence of both Croatia and the Hapsburgs. He wasn't protecting the empire, but rather he hoped that by so doing he would be able to procure certain favours from the Austrians.

The situation became more complicated than had been expected, and in December 1848 Emperor Ferdinand abdicated in favour of his teenage son Franz-Josef I. With the revolution in Hungary finally over (with the help of the Russian Tsar) Jelačić's dream of a 'Slavic Austria' also ended. In August 1849, the Hapsburgs returned to their old ways, with Emperor Franz-Josef I eliminating the new constitution he had formulated and imposing a centralist-absolutist regime accompanied by Germanization that eliminated all political freedom.

One of the National Party's demands that was eventually implemented was the integration of the *Krajina* (military border) into Croatia in 1881, which extended Croatian territory by one-third. This brought a considerable Serb population into the sphere of Croatian politics, a situation that was immediately abused by the new pro-Hungarian ban, Khuen Hedervary (1883-1903), who played off the ongoing competition between Croats and Serbs to weaken the Slav position by inciting conflicts between them. At this time there were 103 Serb representatives in the Croatian parliament, of whom 101 were pro-Hungarian.

On 16 May 1895, during a state visit by Francis Joseph, the Hungarian flag was burnt in Zagreb, reflecting a mood of discontent. Soon after that, the Croatian Peasants' Party, led by Stjepan Radić, entered the Croatian political scene. It represented a sizable force, as about 80% of the population were peasants. All the progressive parties united into one party in 1902, and the so-called Croatian Question, dealing with the destiny of Austro-Hungarian Slavs and the monarchy, moved more and more to the centre of politics.

Meanwhile, in Serbia, King Alexander, of the pro-German Obrenović Dynasty, was assassinated in 1903, and substituted by Petar, of the Karadjordjević Dynasty, which was more orientated towards Russia, France and Britain. The change of dynasty brought about opposition to the Austro-Hungarian Empire within Serbia, and many Serbs in Croatia also stopped supporting Hungary, and switched their interests instead to building closer ties with the Croats.

A series of events, culminating with the assassination of the Austrian Archduke in Sarajevo (organized by a Serbian movement known as the Black Hand, without the knowledge of the Serbian king), led the entire region into the First World War (1914-1918).

During the First World War, the centre of Croatian politics was moved outside the country with the exiled Yugoslav Committee, which represented the Yugoslavian people under the Austro-Hungarian monarchy, and aimed to unify all the South Slav countries into one nation. A very important event, which somehow inspired the idea of a new South Slav nation, was an agreement between the allied forces of the Triple Entente (Britain, France and Russia) and Italy. Formulated in 1915 and known as the London Agreement, it promised a large part of the Croatian coast to Italy, provided Rome entered the war on the Allied side.

The Kingdom of Yugoslavia and Tito's Yugoslavia

At the end of the First World War, the southern Slavs – the Croats and their neighbours the Serbs and Slovenes – set up their own state. On 1 December 1918 this unification was officially announced in Belgrade and the new Kingdom of Serbs, Croats and Slovenes was formed. The only person to oppose the unification was Stjepan Radić, leader of the Croatian Peasants' Party, who said to the Croatian delegation before their journey to Belgrade, "Do not rush yourselves like geese in the fog."

The basic problem with the unification was that it was done unconditionally, leaving Croatia with little state autonomy. The unification came about not only due to the aspiration of South Slavic intellectuals from within the country, but also through the interest of France and Britain to disable German influence and the Bolshevik ideal. Meanwhile, under the Treaty of Rapallo, the Triple Entente awarded Italy the region of Istria, the islands of Cres, Lošinj, Lastovo and Palagruža, the city of Zadar and part of Slovenia, as promised in the London Agreement.

In 1921, on St Vitus Day (28 June), parliament voted for a constitution that was centralistic, and as such could not satisfy the Croats, who were determined to keep some sort of autonomy. The Croatian Peasants' Party opposed the move and tried to obtain the support of several Western European countries, but they approved the politics of Belgrade.

Thus in 1927, the Croatian Peasant's Party, lead by Radić, together with the Independent Democratic Party, lead by Svetozar Pribičević, formed a political coalition named the Peasants' Democratic Coalition. Svetozar Pribičević was a Serbian politician from Croatia who initially supported Yugoslavian centralism, and was one of the people responsible for the unconditional unification. However, he was later disheartened and changed his views. Realizing that there was a danger that the Serbs in Croatia might unite with the Croats, extremist politicians from Belgrade shot at members of the Croatian Peasants' Party in parliament on 20 June 1928. Two members of the party were killed and Stjepan Radić later died of the wounds he had received.

King Aleksandar used the assassination to dismiss the parliament on 6 January 1929, to abolish the constitution and set up a royal dictatorship. In the same year, he changed the country's name to the Kingdom of Yugoslavia, meaning the 'Kingdom of the South Slavs', and divided it into nine governmental regions. The use of the terms Croat, Serb and Slovene, together with their national flags, was prohibited. Exception was made for the Serbian flag, on the grounds that it was also the flag of the Serbian Orthodox Church. In 1931, the king announced the new constitution of the Kingdom of Yugoslavia, without a parliamentary vote.

By this time, around 90% of all higher governmental officials were Serbs, and out of 165 generals, 161 were Serbs and only two were Croats. Out of reaction to the regime, the Bosnian-Croat Ante Pavelić founded the Ustaša movement, which stood for military action against the Kingdom of Yugoslavia, and was supported by extremists in Italy and Hungary. On 9 October 1934, members of this movement assassinated King Aleksandar in Marseille while he was on an official visit to France. After Aleksandar's death, Duke Pavle Karadjordjević was installed as a regent to lead the country in the name of the underage king, Peter.

Even though Duke Pavle was strongly opposed to the Germans, the kingdom was surrounded by Axis Powers, and he therefore felt he had no choice but to join them. In reply to a message from the American president, Franklin Roosevelt, that Yugoslavia should not approach the Germans, the duke said: "It's easy for you big nations a long way away to tell the smaller ones what to do." Two days later, on 27 March 1941, a military putsch took place in Belgrade, organized and paid for with 100,000 pounds in gold by the British secret services.

Once the regency had been removed from power, a new government, led by General Dušan Šimović, was formed. Already on 6 April 1941, Germany and Italy attacked the kingdom. On 10 April, in Zagreb, the Independent State of Croatia (NDH) was proclaimed, with Ante Pavelić as leader. Croatia's independence was at first met with high hopes by the majority of Croats, but when the government gave a large part of the coast to Italy, and began persecuting Serbs, Jews and Gypsies, this support suddenly vanished. The country was divided into two spheres: the south was governed by Italians, and the north by Germans.

As a reaction, the Partisan movement was founded and as the terror enforced by the Italians, Germans and the government increased, so the number of partisans rose. Even though the movement was mainly organized by Communists, members of the Croatian Peasants' Party also participated. The leader of the outlawed Communist Party, Josip Broz, now became the organizer of the largest anti-fascist movement in occupied Europe.

On 8 September 1943, Italy capitulated, and it was decided that both the Treaty of Rapallo from 1920 and the Treaty of Rome from 1941, through which Italy had taken possession of much of the Croatian coast, should be abolished.

Initially, the Allied forces only acknowledged the Yugoslav royal government in exile, based in London, but later the British were the first to help the partisans, having been persuaded by Winston Churchill, who even sent his son as a military agent to Tito. That was how the British established a strong military base on the island of Vis, which for some time was the capital of liberated Yugoslavia. It was on Vis, on 14 June 1944, that the first meeting between Tito and Šubašić, the representative of the Yugoslav government in exile, took place. In early 1945, there was a conference in Yalta, where the well-known division of interests in a liberated Europe was agreed between Stalin and Churchill. Their interests in Yugoslavia were divided 50-50.

Germany capitulated on 9 May 1945, bringing about the end of the Independent State of Croatia. Together with the military retreat, many pro-Ustaša civilians also tried to leave the country, frightened of possible revenge attacks. When they reached Austria, they were turned back by the British army, and regardless of whether they were soldiers or civilians, they were handed over to the partisans and killed on the field of Bleiburg.

The true number of war casualties remains unknown. After the Second World War, the Yugoslavian government sent a report (for obtaining war reparations) to an international committee in which they stated that 1,700,000 people had been killed. But many people believe that the real number was around 1,000,000. Estimates regarding how many people died in the infamous concentration camp of Jasenovac vary from 60,000 to 700,000.

The Federal People's Republic of Yugoslavia was proclaimed on 29 November 1945, organized as a federal and socialist country of people with equal rights. It was made up of six republics (Slovenia, Croatia, Serbia, Montenegro, Macedonia, and Bosnia and Herzegovina), and unlike the other countries of Eastern Europe, did not acknowledge Stalin as holding absolute power, as the Yugoslav partisans had liberated the country from the Germans by themselves.

Yugoslavia now found itself acting as a barrier between the Eastern and Western blocks. Placing itself midway between the Communist East and the Capitalist West, it set up the so-called self-management organizations, in which firms were managed by the workers themselves through a workers' council, which had the power to determine production, to decide on the distribution of profit and to build homes for their workers.

Post-war reconstruction was rapid and optimistic. Increased industrialization brought about mass migration from rural areas to the cities, and modern high-rise suburbs sprung up. Public health and education were well funded, and living standards rose significantly. Tourism began developing along the Adriatic coast in the 1960s, bringing with it foreign currency. All this was conducted under the ideal of 'Brotherhood and Unity', a motto Tito coined to stress the importance of holding the country together and suppressing individual nationalist aspirations.

However, the richer republics (Croatia and Slovenia) soon began to object to having to pay hefty taxes to Belgrade for investment in the less-developed parts of the country. This, plus the fact that national feelings could not be openly expressed, gradually lead to a silent discontent that culminated in the so-called 'Croatian Spring' of 1971. Those who participated demanded greater autonomy for Croatia, greater cultural freedom, and for the foreign currencies received from tourism and earned by Croats working abroad to stay in the republic. By the end of 1971 Tito decided that it had all gone too far and the movement was suppressed. However, some results were gained in 1973 when a new constitution was introduced by which the individual republics' sovereignty was strengthened and their right to eventual independence was acknowledged.

On 4 May 1980, Josip Broz Tito, the persona who had held Yugoslavia together for almost four decades, died in Ljubljana. The respect he had gained abroad was illustrated by the extraordinary line up of world statesmen who attended his funeral, said to have been the largest gathering of its kind in history. Due to his policy of non-alignment and skilful manoeuvres between the East and West, Yugoslavia had gained greater importance and more loans than a country of such proportions and economic development objectively deserved. Tito left behind the proposal of a rotating presidency, whereby each republic would take a turn at leading the country for one year. But as only a charismatic persona such as Tito himself could hold so many different interests and people on one leash, future problems were in store.

The war of independence

In the late 1980s, the appearance of Albanian nationalism in Kosovo gave a good excuse for the programme for a Greater Serbia. Having seized the presidency in Serbia, in 1988 Slobodan Milošević deposed the Communist leaders of Vojvodina, Kosovo and Montenegro, and in 1989 he made amendments to the Serbian constitution, thereby eliminating the autonomy of the provinces of Vojvodina and Kosovo.

The year 1989 saw the fall of the Berlin Wall and the demise of Communist regimes throughout the countries of Eastern Europe, followed the disintegration of the USSR. Attempts by the Croatian economist Ante Marković and the Reformed Communists to save Yugoslavia seemed destined to fail from the start, mainly because of Milošević. In spring 1990, the Croatian Democratic Union (HDZ), lead by Franjo Tudjman, won the elections in Croatia on a nationalist manifesto. The Assembly met for the first time on 30 May 1990, and Tudjman was elected president. However, in August, Serbs in Knin began rebelling against the Croatian state, fearing that they would be marginalized by its nationalist agenda.

During the first months of 1991, the presidents of the six republics of Yugoslavia conducted negotiations about the governmental structure of Yugoslavia. Croatia and Slovenia wanted a confederation, while Milošević insisted on a firm federation. In May 1991, a referendum for independence and sovereignty was held in Croatia, with 93% of those who attended voting in favour (turn out was 82%).

At the end of June, the Yugoslavian People's Army (JNA) was sent in to Slovenia, but fighting there lasted just a few days as the country was not a target of Milošević's expansionism, having no significant Serbian minority. However, the war then transferred to Croatia, where Milošević was eager to defend the 600,000 strong Serbian community, who were mainly concentrated in the old *Krajina* (military border) zones. Local Serbs worked together with the JNA, who were confronted by poorly armed Croatian policemen and voluntary soldiers. Much of the former *Krajina* came under Serb control in the so-called Log Revolution (trees were felled and placed across roads to block access to the region), and the Republic of the Serbian Krajina was declared, effectively cutting off one-third of the country. Basically the Serbs said that if the Croats could claim independence from Belgrade, then they wanted independence from Zagreb.

Serbian TV, Milošević's main propaganda tool, predicted the resurgence of the Independent State of Croatia (NDH), spreading fear among Serbs of a return to the Second World War-style persecution. Likewise, Croatian TV broadcast horrific stories of Serbian barbarianism and the evils of Communism. The seeds of ethnic hatred had been sown and it became increasingly impossible to distinguish the truth from the lies.

Since negotiations with the mediation of the EU proved unsuccessful, the Croatian parliament broke off all relations with Yugoslavia on 8 October 1991. Also in October, the JNA and Montenegran forces placed Dubrovnik under a six-month siege, and in November, after heroic resistance by the Croats, the Serbs managed to take Vukovar in eastern Slavonia in the bloodiest and cruellest fighting the war would see.

Members of the EU, with much persuasion from Germany and the Vatican, recognized Croatia's independence on 15 January 1992. The JNA left Serb-occupied territories, which remained, however, in the hands of the self-proclaimed Republic of the Serbian Krajina. In March 1992 UN peacekeepers were sent in to oversee the situation. Isolated incidents of ethnic violence continued, but all-out fighting had stopped. On 22 May 1992 Croatia became a member of the United Nations.

Under President Clinton, the US began sending in American military advisors to train the Croatian army. In early May 1995, with American blessing, in the military operation Blijesak (Lightning), Croatian forces attacked a Serb-held enclave in western Slavonia. The Serbs were forced to evacuate the region, giving the Croatian army a victory and considerably reducing the Croatian territory controlled by the Serbs.

Then, in August, with the military operation Oluja (Storm), Serb-held areas of North Dalmatia and Lika were liberated. The fall of the Republic of the Serbian Krajina was officially announced when Croatian soldiers hoisted the red and white flag above Knin Fortress. A mass exodus of Serbian families ensued, with most fleeing to neighbouring Bosnia and to Serbia-proper.

Through the Erdut Agreement, the area of eastern Slavonia with Vukovar and Baranja was placed under UN control, until being reintegrated into Croatian territory in January 1998.

Once hostilities were over, it was time to pick up the pieces. Despite having delivered the country its long-desired independence, Tudjman and the ruling HDZ party rapidly lost popularity. The international community accused the Croatian state of interfering with Bosnia (Tudjman had set up an embarrassing allegiance with Bosnian Croats), media manipulation, an appalling human rights record, and the failure to comply with The Hague over war crimes. During the war, Tudjman's upholding of conservative values such as the family, the church and the nation had been enough to keep many people happy.

But after several years of peace, it became apparent that the entire national economy had been undermined, and that nothing would improve until there was a complete change in policy. A new elite class had emerged – those close to the HDZ who had been awarded hefty slices of state property for their loyalty, and those who had made fast money out of black market dealings during the war. The rest of society remained impoverished, unemployment was rife, and even those who had jobs seldom saw their monthly pay cheque on time.

(*This section was researched and written by Domagoj Mijan*).

Croatia today

After the war of independence both Tudjman and Milošević dodged justice: Tudjman died, after a long illness, in December 1999, and Milošević passed away in March 2006, before The Hague was able to pass sentence on either of them.

After Tudjman's death, the HDZ immediately set about trying to organize a convincing election campaign, but the Croatian public had already lost faith. At the elections in January 2000 a new centre-left six-party coalition won and former Communists Ivica Račan and Stipe Mesić were sworn in as Croatia's prime minister and president. However, early elections in November 2003 saw the HDZ back in power, the party having apparently dispelled its nationalist, authoritarian image to become a mainstream conservative movement. Ivo Sanader thus replaced Račan as prime minister.

The new government promised to steer the country towards the European Union and encourage national reconciliation. However, despite much-improved relations with Serbia, and the fact that the Independent Democratic Serbian Party (SDSS), which aims to facilitate the return of refugees, formed a part of Sanader's coalition government, by 2007 only 125,000 of the 250,000 displaced Croatian Serbs had returned to register in Croatia, and most of these were elderly people from rural villages, or people who had registered but were not actually living in Croatia. This slow progress is attributed to problems over property (many Serb homes were destroyed or occupied by other people during the war), unemployment and fear of discrimination.

Another major stumbling block, up until late 2005, was Croatia's failure to hand over indicted war criminals to the Criminal Tribunal for the Former Yugoslavia (ICTY) in The Hague. The key to Croatia commencing EU accession negotiations was the capture of General Ante Gotovina (indicted for crimes during and after Operation Storm in 1995, but considered by extreme Croatians nationalists to be a hero). In December 2005, Gotovina was arrested in Spain and handed over to The Hague (and consequently sentenced to 24 years in prison in 2011). In 2005 and 2006, President Mesić of Croatia and President Tadić of Serbia exchanged official visits in a bid to improve relations between the two countries.

Sanader's government was narrowly re-elected in November 2007. In July 2009, he resigned unexpectedly (and has since been charged with corruption and sentenced to 10 years in prison), and was replaced by Croatia's first female prime minister, Jadranka Kosor. In November 2009, Jadranka Kosor and her Slovenian counterpart Borut Pahor signed an agreement ending Slovenia's blockade of Croatia's EU accession. Slovenia, which was the first former Yugoslav state to join the EU in 2004, had been blocking Zagreb's progress due to land and maritime border disputes, which still need to be resolved. Mesić remained president until January 2010, when his maximum two five-year terms in office came to an end. Following a tense presidential campaign, the Croatian people voted Josip Josipović as their new President.

Josipović, a left-wing law professor and classical music composer, promised to fight corruption and bring the country into the European Union. His victory was welcomed by Serbian President Boris Tadić, and he is expected to improve Croatia's relations with the other countries of former Yugoslavia. Croatia now hopes to enter the EU in January 2012.

In December 2011, a general election ousted the HDZ, and heralded in a new centre-left coalition named Kukuriku (translating literally to "cock-a-doodle-doo", suggesting a wake-up call, in tribute to Kukuriku, a slow-food restaurant just outside Rijeka, see Restaurants, page 53). Led by present Prime Minister Zoran Milanović, the coalition promises to tackle the ailing economy, unemployment, corruption and organized crime.

Another suprise was in store in November 2012 when the appeals panel at The Hague retracted the verdict (3:2) on Ante Gotovina's crimes against humanity during Operation Storm, bringing about his immediate release, and putting new strains on relations between Croatia and Serbia.

A national referendum on EU accession was held in Croatia in January 2012, with 66% of participants voting in favour (though turnout was only 44%). At the time of writing, Croatia is on course to become the 28th member of the EU on 1 July 2013.

Art and architecture

Painting and sculpture

The first individual artists to have been recorded in the history of Croatian art were sculptors working in Romanesque style during the 13th century: Master Radovan, who completed the magnificent main portal of Trogir Cathedral, and Andrea Buvina, who carved the well-preserved wooden doors to Split Cathedral. Then, during the 15th century, with the dawn of the Renaissance, some important artists combined the skills of architecture and sculpture, notably Juraj Dalmatinac, who was responsible for the 74 heads cut in stone that make up the freize on the exterior of Šibenik Cathedral, and his pupil Andrea Aleši, who completed the delicately carved baptistry in the same building.

The 15th century also saw the first notable Croatian movement of painters. In the wealthy and culturally advanced city of Dubrovnik, a group of painters inspired by Italian Gothic art and the Byzantine tradition became known as the Dubrovnik School. Unfortunately, few of their works have been preserved – mainly due to the destructive earthquake of 1667 – but Blaž Jurjev Trogiranin (also known as Blasius Pictor) from Trogir and Lovro Dobričević from Kotor (present-day Montenegro) can be singled out. They produced a wealth of icons and ornate polyptychs featuring religious scenes, both for Catholic and Orthodox churches, using rich blues, greens and reds, often against a golden background. Today you can see examples of Trogiranin's work in Korčula Town – a polyptych *Our Lady with Saints* in the Abbey Treasury and a polyptych *Our Lady the Co-redeemer* in the Church of All Saints. Several outstanding pieces by Dobričević are on display in the Dominican Monastery in Dubrovnik.

The country's most noted 19th-century painter is Vlaho Bukovac (1855-1922). Born in Cavtat, he studied in Paris and also spent some time in England, where he executed portraits of various aristocratic families, into which he was received as a friend and guest; his *Potiphar's Wife* was exhibited in the Royal Academy of London. From 1903 to 1922 he was a professor at the Academy of Art in Prague. The house were he was born in Cavtat has been turned into a gallery displaying a collection of his paintings and drawings.

Split's greatest painter is generally acknowledged to be Emanuel Vidović (1870-1953). He studied in Venice then moved back to Split, where he would work outdoors, making colourful sketches, then return to his studio to rework his impressions on large canvasses, often producing dark, hazy paintings with a slightly haunting atmosphere. The Vidović Gallery in Split displays almost 70 of his paintings, donated to the city by his family.

For many people, Croatia's most outstanding 20th-century artist is Edo Murtić (1921-2005). Born in Velika Pisanica near Bjelovar in inland Croatia, he grew up in Zagreb where he also studied art. During the Second World War he designed posters and illustrated books connected to the Partisan liberation movement. After the war he visited New York, where he met American abstract expressionists such as Jackson Pollock, and completed a cycle of paintings called Impressions of America. During the 1960s and 1970s he was one of the masters of European abstract art, painting vast canvasses with mighty bold strokes and daring colours. In the 1980s his works became less abstract, featuring recognizable Mediterranean landscapes. He has paintings in the Tate Gallery in London and MOMA in New York.

Croatia's best-known and most prolific 20th-century sculptor has to be Ivan Meštrovi (1883-1962). Born into a peasant family from the Dalmatian hinterland, he was sent to work with a stonecutter in Split, where he showed considerable skill and was thus sent to study at the Art Academy in Vienna, financed by a Viennese mine owner. Although he did not like his professor, he had great respect for the noted Austrian architect Otto Wagner, who also taught there, and soon became influenced by the Vienna Secession movement. In Vienna he also met Rodin, who inspired him to travel in Italy and France, and then to settle in Paris, where he became internationally renowned. He then spent several years in Rome, mixing with members of the Italian Futurist movement, such as Ungaretti and de Chirico. In 1911 he won first prize at an international exhibition in Rome, where critics hailed him as the best sculptor since the Renaissance.

During the First World War he spent some time in England where he staged a one-man exhibition at London's Victoria and Albert Museum. After the First World War he returned to his homeland, taking a house in Zagreb – which is now open to the public as the Meštrović Atelier – and designing a villa in Split, today the Meštrović Gallery. However, at the beginning of the Second World War he was imprisoned by the fascist Ustaše, and it was only through the intervention of his friends in Italy, including the Pope, that he managed to leave the country. He spent the rest of his life in the USA, but upon his death his body was returned to Croatia where he was buried in the family mausoleum as he had requested. Today he has pieces in stone, bronze and wood on show in the Tate Gallery in London and the Uffizi in Florence. In several Croatian towns you can see bronze statues of important local cultural figures, such as Grgur Ninski and Marko Marulić in Split and Juraj Dalmatinac in Šibenik, which he created as public works. In the US his best-known outdoor piece is *Equestrian Indians* in Grant Park, Chicago.

Architecture

Classical
The finest remaining buildings from Roman times can be seen in the cities of Pula and Split. In the former, the oldest significant monument is a first-century BC triumphal arch, known as the Arch of the Sergi. It was built to celebrate the role of three high-ranking military officers from the Sergi family at the Battle of Actium in 31 BC; upon their return home they would have led their triumphant soldiers through the arch into the walled city. Made up of a single arch flanked with slender columns with Corinthian capitals, it is ornamented with base reliefs of dolphins, a sphinx and a griffon, and an eagle struggling with a snake. Originally it would have been topped with statues of the three generals. Italian Renaissance architects Palladio and Michelangelo were obviously suitably impressed by it, as both sketched it on their travels. Close by, the present-day main square was once the forum and, of the principal public buildings that stood here, the first-century AD Temple of Augustus remains intact. Typically designed to be viewed from the front, it is elevated on a high base with steps leading up to an open portico supported by six tall columns. Located outside the former walls, Pula's best-known Roman building is the colossal first-century AD amphitheatre, which was built to host gladiator fights and could accommodate up to 22,000 spectators, making it the sixth largest surviving Roman amphitheatre in the world.

Moving south down the coast, Split grew up within the 25-m-high walls of a unique third-century palace, commissioned by Emperor Diocletian as a retirement residence. Combining the qualities of a Roman garrison and an imperial villa, this vast structure is based on a rectangular ground plan measuring 215 m by 180 m, and contains various individual monuments such as an octagonal mausoleum (now the cathedral) and a classical temple dedicated to Jupiter (now a baptistery). British and French architects and artists first acknowledged its magnificence during the 18th century when many visited it as part of the Grand Tour; it is said to have inspired the Scottish architect Robert Adam in some of his finest neoclassical projects upon his return to the UK.

Some 6 km inland from Split, the archaeological site of Salona was once the largest Roman urban centre in Croatia, with an estimated population of 60,000 in the third century AD. Sadly it was devastated in the seventh century; today only the ruins remain.

During the sixth century the coastal region came under Byzantine rule. Architecturally, the Byzantine Empire is best known for its magnificent Christian basilicas, and the most outstanding example in Croatia is Euphrasius Basilica in Poreč. Built under the rule of Emperor Justinian (AD 483-565), during the same period as Hagia Sophia in Constantinople (present-day Istanbul), this complex comprises a central atrium, with an octagonal baptistery to one side, and opposite it the basilica itself, where the central aisle focuses on a main apse decorated with splendid golden mosaics.

Pre-Romanesque

The Croats arrived in the region in the seventh century and gradually began taking on the Christian faith. Between the ninth and 11th centuries about 150 small pre-Romanesque churches, often referred to as early Croatian churches, were built, mainly along the coast. Byzantine influence is apparent in their geometric massing, though they tend towards minimum decoration, limited to finely carved stonework ornamented with plait-design motifs reminiscent of Celtic art. The most perfect example is the tiny ninth-century Holy Cross in Nin, based on the plan of a Greek cross, while the largest and most imposing is the monumental ninth-century rotonda St Donat's in Zadar, based on a circular ground plan with three semi-circular apses. You can see an excellent collection of early Croatian church stonework in the Croatian Museum of Archaeological Monuments in Split.

Romanesque

The 12th century saw the dawn of the Romanesque age, which was marked by imposing cathedrals, generally made up of triple naves with semi-circular apses, and ornate façades featuring blind arches. The most beautiful – the Cathedral of St Anastasia and the Church of St Chrysogonus – are in Zadar, though other notables examples include the Cathedral of Our Lady of the Assumption in Krk Town, the Church of St Mary the Great (which was a cathedral until 1828) in Rab Town, and the portal of the Cathedral of St Lawrence in Trogir, which was carved by the outstanding Dalmatian sculptor Master Radovan in the early 13th century. Unfortunately, Croatia's two most important Romanesque cathedrals were destroyed – the one in Zagreb by the Tartars in 1242, and the one in Dubrovnik by the 1667 earthquake (subsequently rebuilt in later styles).

Venetian Gothic

When Venice began colonizing the east Adriatic coast, it brought with it the so-called Venetian Gothic style, characterized by the pointed arch and rib vaulting. The style is apparent in 15th- and 16th-century churches and houses in Istria and Dalmatia, such as the finely carved portal of Korčula Cathedral by Bonino from Milan, and the triple pointed-arch windows of the Čipko Palace in Trogir by Andrea Aleši. It is often seen mixed with more severe Renaissance elements, most notably in the work of Juraj Dalmatinac on Šibenik Cathedral (see below), hence the term Gothic-Renaissance.

Renaissance

The Renaissance, which started in Italy, marked a revival of Roman civilization, not just in art and architecture but in an entire set of values. The movement is normally said to have dawned in Croatia in 1441, when Juraj Dalmatinac, a builder from Zadar who had trained for a short time in Venice, began work on Šibenik Cathedral (although he did not live to see it completed; the later work was carried out by two of his pupils, Nikola Firentinac and Andrija Aleši). Dalmatinac also drew up the urban plan for Pag Town in 1443, and worked on other noted projects, such as the Chapel of St Anastasius in Split Cathedral and Minceta Fortress in Dubrovnik. You can see a 20th-century statue of Dalmatinac, by Ivan Meštrović, in front of Šibenik Cathedral.

The Renaissance continued developing along the coast, in areas that were not under the Turks, until the end of the 16th century. During this period many towns were fortified with defensive walls and towers, the best examples being Dubrovnik, Korčula and Hvar.

Increased wealth, plus the ideals of Renaissance philosophy, lead to the construction of more sophisticated houses, with refined details such as carved doors and window frames, balconies with balustrades, stone washbasins, decorated fireplaces and built-in cupboards. People became interested in the relationship between man and nature; houses were set in gardens with arcaded walkways, fountains and stone benches, the best examples being Tvrdalj in Stari Grad on the island of Hvar and Trsteno Arboretum near Dubrovnik, both from the 16th century.

Baroque

Regarded as a symbol of Western civilization, and therefore the antithesis of Ottoman culture, the baroque style flourished in northern Croatia during the late 17th and 18th centuries. The Jesuits, who played an important part in reinforcing the Roman Catholic faith in areas threatened by the Turks, were responsible for introducing the grandiose, curvilinear baroque style to the region. As the Turks were gradually pushed out, many buildings were constructed, reconstructed or extended in baroque style.

Today, the best-preserved baroque town centre is in Varaždin; tragically Vukovar, formerly regarded as the finest baroque town in Croatia, was all but devastated during the war of independence during the 1990s. Other notable examples can be found in Osijek (the 18th-century Tvrđa complex) and in Dubrovnik (the Cathedral from 1671 and the Jesuit Church from 1725, both designed by Italian architects during reconstruction following the earthquake of 1667).

Eclectic

During the 19th century, eclectic design – the revival and reinterpretation of past styles – was popular throughout Europe. In Zagreb, the buildings of Donji Grad, constructed when the region was under Austro-Hungary, mix various elements from classical, Gothic and baroque periods. The most prolific architect in north Croatia at this time was Herman Bolle (1845-1926). Born in Koln, Germany, he participated in the construction of about 140 buildings in Croatia, including Zagreb Cathedral, Mirogoj Cemetery and the Museum of Arts and Crafts, all in Zagreb.

Vienna Secession

By the close of the 19th century, artists and architects in various parts of Europe were rebelling against the decadence of eclectic buildings and the pomp and formality of older styles, and searching instead for more pure and functional forms. In German-speaking countries this trend was known as Jugendstil, and in France as art nouveau. In 1897 in Vienna, a group of visual artists founded a movement, which became known as the Vienna Secession. The architects involved strove to give simple geometric forms to their buildings, while working in close collaboration with artists, who provided discreet, elegant details such as frescoes and mosaics. The best examples of this style in Croatia, which was still part of the Austro-Hungarian Empire at the time, are Villa Santa Maria, Villa Frappart and Villa Magnolia, all designed by the Austrian architect Carl Seidl and found in Lovran, close to Opatija. In Osijek, Europska Avenue is lined with fine Viennese Secessionist buildings by local architects.

Modernism

There are very few examples of quality modernist architecture in Croatia, though the ideals of the modern movement were held dear by the Socialist state during the second half of the 20th century. The resulting buildings are primarily high-rise apartment blocks, most of which are light and airy with large balconies, and vast hotel complexes that have sprung up along the coast, which are rather impersonal but functional and comfortable.

Contents

Footnotes

Language

Croatian belongs to the South Slavic branch of the Slavic group of languages – a similar language is spoken by Serbs, Montenegrins and Bosnians. Most people working in tourism, as well as the majority of younger Croatians, speak good English, so you won't have much of a problem communicating unless you get off the beaten track. If you do make the effort to learn a few words and phrases, though, your efforts are likely to be rewarded with a smile of appreciation.

Vowels

a	like 'a' in cat
e	like 'e' in vet
i	like 'i' in sip
o	like 'o' in fox
u	like 'ou' in soup

Consonants

c	like 'ts' in bats
č	like 'ch' in cheese
ć	like 'ch' in future
đ	like 'j' in jeans
dž	like 'dj' in adjust
j	like 'y' in yes
lj	like 'ly' in billion
nj	like 'ny' in canyon
š	like 'sh' in push

Numbers

1	jedan (ye-dan)
2	dva (dva)
3	tri (tree)
4	četri (che-ti-ree)
5	pet (pet)
6	šest (shest)
7	sedam (se-dam)
8	osam (o-sam)
9	devet (de-vet)
10	deset (de-set)
11	jedanest (ye-'da-na-est)
12	dvanaest ('dva-na-est)
20	dvadeset ('dva-de-set)
50	pedeset (pe-'de'set)
100	sto (sto)

Basics

yes	da (da)
no	ne (ne)
please	molim (mo-lim)
thank you	hvala (hva-la)
hello	bog (bog)
goodbye	dovidjenja (do-vee-'jen-ya)
excuse me	oprostite (o-'pro-sti-te)
sorry	pardon (par-don)
that's OK	u redu je (oo re-doo ye)
to	u (oo)
from	iz (iz)
I (don't) speak Croatian	ja (ne) govorim Hrvatski (Yah ne 'go-vo-rim 'hr-vat-ski)
do you speak English?	govorite li vi engleski? (go-vo-ri-te li 'en-gle-ski?)
good morning	dobro jutro (do-bro yoo-tro)
good afternoon	dobar dan (do-bar dan)
good evening	dobro večer (do-bra ve-cher)
good night	laku noć (la-koo noch)
my name is…	moje ime je… (mo-ye ime ye…)

Questions

how	kako (ka-ko)
when	kada (ka-da)
where	gdje (g-dyay)
why	zašto (za-shto)
what	što (shto)

Time

morning	*jutro (yoo-tro)*
afternoon	*popodne (po-'po-dne)*
evening	*večer (ve-cher)*
night	*noć (noch)*
yesterday	*jučer (yoo-cher)*
today	*danas (da-nas)*
tomorrow	*sutra (soo-tra)*
what time is it?	*koliko je sati?*
	('ko-li-ko ye sa-ti?)
it is…	*točno… (toch-no…)*
0900	*devet sati (de-vet sa-ti)*
midday	*podne (po-dne)*
midnight	*ponoć (po-noch)*

Days

Monday	*Ponedjeljak*
	(Po-'ne-diel-yak)
Tuesday	*Utorak ('Oo-to-rak)*
Wednesday	*Srijeda (Sree-ye-da)*
Thursday	*Četvrtak (Che-'tvr-tak)*
Friday	*Petak (Pe-tak)*
Saturday	*Subota ('Soo-bo-ta)*
Sunday	*Nedjelja ('Ne-dyel-ya)*

Signs and notices

Airport	*Aerodrom*
Entrance/Exit	*Ulaz/Izlaz*
No smoking	*Zabranjeno pušenje*
Toilets	*WC*
Ladies/Gentlemen	*Ženski/Muški*

Index

Titles available in the Footprint *Focus* range

Latin America	UK RRP	US RRP
Bahia & Salvador	£7.99	$11.95
Brazilian Amazon	£7.99	$11.95
Brazilian Pantanal	£6.99	$9.95
Buenos Aires & Pampas	£7.99	$11.95
Cartagena & Caribbean Coast	£7.99	$11.95
Costa Rica	£8.99	$12.95
Cuzco, La Paz & Lake Titicaca	£8.99	$12.95
El Salvador	£5.99	$8.95
Guadalajara & Pacific Coast	£6.99	$9.95
Guatemala	£8.99	$12.95
Guyana, Guyane & Suriname	£5.99	$8.95
Havana	£6.99	$9.95
Honduras	£7.99	$11.95
Nicaragua	£7.99	$11.95
Northeast Argentina & Uruguay	£8.99	$12.95
Paraguay	£5.99	$8.95
Quito & Galápagos Islands	£7.99	$11.95
Recife & Northeast Brazil	£7.99	$11.95
Rio de Janeiro	£8.99	$12.95
São Paulo	£5.99	$8.95
Uruguay	£6.99	$9.95
Venezuela	£8.99	$12.95
Yucatán Peninsula	£6.99	$9.95

Asia	UK RRP	US RRP
Angkor Wat	£5.99	$8.95
Bali & Lombok	£8.99	$12.95
Chennai & Tamil Nadu	£8.99	$12.95
Chiang Mai & Northern Thailand	£7.99	$11.95
Goa	£6.99	$9.95
Gulf of Thailand	£8.99	$12.95
Hanoi & Northern Vietnam	£8.99	$12.95
Ho Chi Minh City & Mekong Delta	£7.99	$11.95
Java	£7.99	$11.95
Kerala	£7.99	$11.95
Kolkata & West Bengal	£5.99	$8.95
Mumbai & Gujarat	£8.99	$12.95

Africa & Middle East	UK RRP	US RRP
Beirut	£6.99	$9.95
Cairo & Nile Delta	£8.99	$12.95
Damascus	£5.99	$8.95
Durban & KwaZulu Natal	£8.99	$12.95
Fès & Northern Morocco	£8.99	$12.95
Jerusalem	£8.99	$12.95
Johannesburg & Kruger National Park	£7.99	$11.95
Kenya's Beaches	£8.99	$12.95
Kilimanjaro & Northern Tanzania	£8.99	$12.95
Luxor to Aswan	£8.99	$12.95
Nairobi & Rift Valley	£7.99	$11.95
Red Sea & Sinai	£7.99	$11.95
Zanzibar & Pemba	£7.99	$11.95

Europe	UK RRP	US RRP
Bilbao & Basque Region	£6.99	$9.95
Brittany West Coast	£7.99	$11.95
Cádiz & Costa de la Luz	£6.99	$9.95
Granada & Sierra Nevada	£6.99	$9.95
Languedoc: Carcassonne to Montpellier	£7.99	$11.95
Málaga	£5.99	$8.95
Marseille & Western Provence	£7.99	$11.95
Orkney & Shetland Islands	£5.99	$8.95
Santander & Picos de Europa	£7.99	$11.95
Sardinia: Alghero & the North	£7.99	$11.95
Sardinia: Cagliari & the South	£7.99	$11.95
Seville	£5.99	$8.95
Sicily: Palermo & the Northwest	£7.99	$11.95
Sicily: Catania & the Southeast	£7.99	$11.95
Siena & Southern Tuscany	£7.99	$11.95
Sorrento, Capri & Amalfi Coast	£6.99	$9.95
Skye & Outer Hebrides	£6.99	$9.95
Verona & Lake Garda	£7.99	$11.95

North America	UK RRP	US RRP
Vancouver & Rockies	£8.99	$12.95

Australasia	UK RRP	US RRP
Brisbane & Queensland	£8.99	$12.95
Perth	£7.99	$11.95

For the latest books, e-books and a wealth of travel information, visit us at:
www.footprinttravelguides.com.

footprinttravelguides.com

Join us on facebook for the latest travel news, product releases, offers and amazing competitions:
www.facebook.com/footprintbooks.